Blurred Vision

Aaron "Woogy" Wolgamott

WestBow
PRESS
A DIVISION OF THOMAS NELSON

WestBow Press books may be ordered through booksellers or by contacting:

WestBow Press
A Division of Thomas Nelson
1663 Liberty Drive
Bloomington, IN 47403
www.westbowpress.com
1-(866) 928-1240

Because of the dynamic nature of the Internet, any web addresses or links contained in this book may have changed since publication and may no longer be valid. The views expressed in this work are solely those of the author and do not necessarily reflect the views of the publisher, and the publisher hereby disclaims any responsibility for them.

Any people depicted in stock imagery provided by Thinkstock are models, and such images are being used for illustrative purposes only.

Certain stock imagery © Thinkstock.

ISBN: 978-1-4497-4627-8 (sc)
ISBN: 978-1-4497-4628-5 (e)

Library of Congress Control Number: 2012906158

Printed in the United States of America

WestBow Press rev. date: 4/10/2012

To my wife and best friend, Charissa

Contents

Introduction

I have been in the church and the ministry for what seems like my whole life. My parents have been involved in ministry in different capacities since I was a kid, and when I was old enough, I began to get involved in ministry as well. After high school, I went to college to become a youth pastor, and after graduation I began my first full-time ministry job. Ministry and the church have defined a major portion of my life, and in my years of being in the church, I had come to notice that there are many in the church who have misunderstandings and misconceptions of what it means to be a follower of Christ.

A few years back, as I was doing my yearly planning for the upcoming school year, I felt led to do a series of lessons to address several well-known aspects of the Christian life that I believed many in the church might have gotten wrong in some way. The idea behind this series of lessons was to challenge my students to not just do what they have seen and what has always been done when it comes to following Christ, but instead to seek the truth of Scripture and apply what they find to how they live to ensure they are truly following Christ. I called that series of lessons *Blurred Vision*.

As my youth group was going through this series of lessons, I began to get a feeling that I should be writing them down in more detail than I normally do. At the same time, my intern also told me that this was a message more people should hear. It seemed as though

God was leading me to share this lesson series in book form. So I began to keep more detailed notes of my lessons, and I used other speaking opportunities to speak about these ideas more, working through them in different ways to organize my thoughts.

After a while I sat down and began to write it all out. It was exciting, mostly because I knew it wasn't just something I wanted to do, but was rather something God was leading me to do. It was also exciting because it was much bigger than me, something that was outside my comfort zone. The whole process, from writing to publishing, has been an amazing journey, as I have seen God bring it from an idea to publication on his terms and in his own way—I was just along for the ride.

So here it is, the book that began as a series of lessons to challenge my students. My prayer is that the message of this book will be a challenge to you as well as you read it. God has used these messages and the writing process to challenge me and teach me many things, and I know he wants to speak to you, too, as you read this.

As you read this book and the messages within it, there are two questions that I want you to keep in the forefront of your mind, both to think about and to answer—two questions that will hopefully challenge you and cause you to see what God wants to tell you.

1. Am I willing to allow my blurred vision to be cleared up so that I may see the truth?
2. Once I see the truth, how will I live my life according to it?

As followers of Christ, we need to do just that: follow Christ. Knowing what Jesus taught us, what the Bible says, and how to live godly lives is all worthless if we don't apply that knowledge and live accordingly. We must live it, not just know it.

May this book challenge, renew, and bless you.

Perspective

Perspective is the way in which a person views life. Our perspectives are based upon many different influences in our lives—where we live, our family and friends, our experiences, what we both choose to believe and are taught to believe, etc. These very perspectives shape who we are and the choices we make.

I am an American—the oldest son in a family of four kids. I grew up moving a lot, and football has been a big part of my life since I was little. I've been raised to view things a certain way, based on the culture in which I was brought up in and the environment by which I was surrounded. We have all been raised in certain cultures and environments by certain people who have certain views of things. And those views, or perspectives, influence our way of thinking and viewing things.

We have also made choices on our own to view and think about things a certain way based on what we want, what we've seen and heard, what we choose to believe, and how we'd like our lives to be directed. These choices lead us to have certain views and perspectives that shape how we think and act, how we see and understand the world around us, and how we make decisions and life choices.

I am also a follower of Christ, and that brings in a whole new set of perspectives. When I read the Bible, I find that God's point of view is often totally different from the views of this world. Because

I am a follower of Christ, I need to adopt God's point of view. Yet because I'm from and live in this world, I am influenced by the views of this world.

Living a godly life here on this earth can be difficult because of the struggle between the views of the world and God's point view. But in order to live for God and be godly people, we need to see things from his point of view.

Yet all too often, we as followers of Christ try to live for God using the world's views and understanding. However, we can't do that and truly live a godly life that is pleasing to God. To live for God—really live for him—we have to see things from God's point of view.

We must change our ways of thinking and understanding, as well as our perspectives, in order to truly live the lives God has called us to. We need to understand that the way this world thinks goes against God the majority of the time. But we have been raised in this world and have minds that were shaped by this world. So we must allow God to transform our minds so that we think differently than the world and the same as God.

To live for God completely, we have to have his point of view and understanding of things. Until then, our vision is blurred.

I attended college at Grace University in Omaha, Nebraska. In Nebraska, during the spring and summer months, you often get storms that are capable of producing tornadoes; it is just part of living in that area of the country. When you live there, you get used to hearing sirens going off and having to go hide in a basement … although I've always been one to run to the window or outside to see if I can get a glimpse of the tornado. (My wife hates when I do that.)

One spring, while I was in college, I had a friend who needed to get home to visit her family. Because the drive was several hours and she was a friend of mine, I agreed to go on this trip with her to help drive. I've always enjoyed road trips and find driving relaxing, so I thought it would be fun.

After driving a while, I began to notice that a storm was beginning to roll in. Severe storms can sometimes come in very quickly out in the Midwest, and that is exactly what was happening this time. The formerly clear sky became clouded, and the warm air began to cool. The longer I drove, the more I noticed that the sky continued to get darker and darker.

As I mentioned earlier, I liked to look for tornadoes, so I've never been one to easily get scared because of a possible tornado. However, with how quickly the sky was growing darker, I was beginning to worry. I began to get a very eerie feeling—the kind of feeling that you can get when a severe storm like this hits. As I continued to drive, it became harder and harder to see because of the increasing darkness. In fact, it got so bad that I was eventually leaning forward in my seat with my chin basically on the steering wheel so that I could see out the windshield to be able to drive.

As I drove like this, my friend was just sitting calmly in the passenger seat next to me. When she looked over to see me driving the way I was, she got a weird look on her face and asked me why I was driving like that. She then did something I had never even thought to do—she pushed the defrost button. As the windshield began to clear up, I was able to see out the windshield a lot better. There was a storm, but it was not nearly as dark and eerie as I had thought it was when I was looking out through a fogged windshield. I felt like such an idiot! And what's worse, I was probably making it even harder to see out by leaning forward, because I was breathing on the windshield, causing it to fog up more.

As I was driving, my vision was completely blurred, because the windshield through which I looked at the outside world was blurred. But once the blurriness was taken away, the truth of the situation was revealed.

Often, we, as Christ-followers, try to live for God in this world using our worldly perspectives. The only way to truly live for God completely is to see things from his perspective—to look at things through his eyes, not ours. We need to remove how we see things as humans so that we can see the truth.

We need to be transformed in our minds by having God's perspective replace our perspectives. We need to see ourselves as followers of Christ who live on earth as opposed to humans who follow Christ. Once we've been transformed by renewing our mindsets, we'll be able to fully follow God, because we will think as he does, and thus we will be able to know and follow what his will for us is. It says in Romans 12:2, "Do not conform any longer to the pattern of this world, but be transformed by the renewing of your mind. Then you will be able to test and approve what God's will is—his good, pleasing and perfect will" (NIV).

All too often, we followers of Christ try to figure out this life and how to live for God in this world on our own strength and with our own knowledge. We know that the Bible is the Word of God and that everything we need for knowing how to live godly lives is given to us in there, yet we still seem to think we can figure it out on our own using our own wisdom and mind-sets.

Unfortunately, because of that kind of thinking, we are now at a place where many who claim to be followers of Christ don't even read the Bible for themselves very often. We are at a time in history where we have more resources and information at our fingertips than ever before. There is so much at our disposal that every single follower of Christ should be able to prepare some sort of a Bible study or lesson to teach, even if he or she doesn't have the gift of teaching. Yet the fact is that despite all those resources and information, a large portion of those who claim to be followers of Christ are ignorant and clueless to the truth of Scripture.

As a youth pastor, my passion, desire, and goal is to train and develop students to own their faith and maintain their own spiritual growth. I'm not looking to create more followers who are in constant need of feeding. I want both students and parents to get to the place where they are capable of feeding themselves spiritually because they read and study their Bibles.

I would love to get to the point where I as a pastor simply turn my students and parents loose to lead lessons, teach small groups, etc. As a pastor, I should always be giving my job away to others who've grown in their faith.

One summer as I attended summer camp with my youth group, I heard the camp speaker say something to the effect of, "Why should I or your youth pastors give you more information or do deeper studies with you when you don't remember or apply what we've already taught you?" Ouch! It sounds kind of harsh, but it's very true.

Hebrews 5:11–14 says, "We have much to say about this, but it is hard to explain because you are slow to learn. In fact, though by this time you ought to be teachers, you need someone to teach you the elementary truths of God's word all over again. You need milk, not solid food! Anyone who lives on milk, being still an infant, is not acquainted with the teaching about righteousness. But solid food is for the mature, who by constant use have trained themselves to distinguish good from evil" (NIV).

The writer of Hebrews seems to be passionately bothered by this. The writer says that you should be teachers by now, sharing what you've learned and studied with others, but you aren't. In fact, instead of being where you should be, you have to be taught the basics all over again. Probably the most disturbing part of what the writer says is, "Anyone who lives on milk, being still an infant, is not acquainted with the teaching about righteousness." If we aren't growing in our faith, if we remain babies rather than maturing, then we won't be able to fully know or understand how to live a godly life.

It's time we followers of Christ changed our perspectives. We need to get rid of our human eyes, cultural eyes, and any other sets of eyes we have. We need get rid of them so that we can have the eyes of Jesus; we need to know the Bible and what it says and actually apply it to our lives. We must stop looking like ignorant morons in a world that hates Jesus, and we must start living out our faith every day. We must start to practice what we preach and let the Bible become our only guide for life.

There is a quote from Brennan Manning that says, "The greatest single cause of atheism in the world today is Christians who acknowledge Jesus with their lips, then walk out the door and deny him by their lifestyle. That is what an unbelieving world simply finds unbelievable."

We as followers of Christ must live as though we are truly following Christ, and that requires that we live our lives according to the truths of God found in Scripture. We must live godly lives so that when the world looks at us, they won't see us, but rather will see Jesus and will be unable to deny his existence and presence in our lives. Like it says in 1 Peter 2:12, "Live such good lives among the pagans that, though they accuse you of doing wrong, they may see your good deeds and glorify God on the day he visits us"(NIV).

It's time for followers of Christ to stop living like the world. It's time for followers of Christ to replace their worldly perspectives with a godly one so that we may begin to truly live for Christ the way God intended. It's time to clear up the misunderstandings and misconceptions, both within and outside of the church.

Christianity

There are two very big misconceptions about Christianity today, both in the church and in the world. As the church, we need to get back to what the Bible says so that we will know the truth and see things from God's point of view. Then we can correctly show the world what the church and Christians are supposed to look like, and thus they will see clearly who God really is.

First Misconception: Jesus Founded a Religion Called Christianity.

If you actually read the four Gospels that document the life of Jesus (Matthew, Mark, Luke, and John), there is never a single mention of him starting a religion. Jesus was called the Son of God, the same God we read of in the Old Testament. John 1:1–2 says, "In the beginning was the Word, and the Word was with God, and the Word was God. He was with God in the beginning."(NIV) "The Word" refers to Jesus, who was around in the Old Testament—and even before that as well.

When Jesus came to earth and began his ministry, he wasn't seeking to create a new religion or belief system. He didn't hope to be the founder of a social movement or club. He came to teach and explain what the Law and the prophets had been telling us for thousands of years in the Old Testament. He came to show us how to live a lifestyle of love that is pleasing to God. He came to undo what the religious leaders had done by turning living for God into a list of dos and don'ts instead of a lifestyle. And he came to fulfill the Law that was impossible for us to fulfill on our own.

There is a book by Don Everts called *Jesus with Dirty Feet*. In it, there is a phrase that says, paraphrased, Jesus was not a Christian, and Jesus never called people to be Christians—he simply called people to follow him.

The practical definition of the word *Christian* is someone who follows Christ so closely that he or she begins to look and act like him. The word *Christian* was first used to describe those who were a part of the early church in Antioch. It was not those in the church who called themselves Christians; it was those outside the church who called them Christians. Those in the world watched these people who were following the teachings of Christ, and they looked and acted so much like Jesus (and they would know, because many had seen him firsthand) that they began to call them "Christ ones," which later became the term *Christians*.

However, that definition and understanding of what it means to be a Christian has been all but forgotten. Today the term *Christian* is often little more than a label or badge to wear. I have heard countless people use the term *Christian* to describe themselves, yet I saw no evidence of them actually following Jesus, let alone looking and acting just like him.

What is amazing is that you couldn't get away with that in other areas of life. Let me give you an example. When a woman says she is pregnant, there is proof. She goes through a nine-month period during which you can see physical changes. And the end result is a new life. If a woman walked around claiming to be pregnant yet without any proof, she would be called a crazy liar. But when someone walks around claiming to be a Christian yet has no proof of that in his or her life, we let it go.

What makes people true followers of Christ isn't their words; it's their actions. It is evident in every aspect of their lives. A follower of Christ takes seriously the command in Ephesians 5:1 to be an imitator of Christ. Followers of Christ understands that they are to be mirror images of Jesus to a lost and dying world that needs him, and they are called to be the ones to take the message of Jesus' love to that world, both in word and through action.

One of my all-time favorite movies is *The Patriot* with Mel Gibson. In this movie about America's fight for freedom, there is a scene in which Gabriel (son of Benjamin Martin and one of the main characters in the movie) goes into a church in South Carolina to enlist as many men willing to volunteer for this fight. When no one is willing, Anne (who later becomes Gabriel's wife) stands up and calls people out. She reminds all the men of the town how they love to talk about independence and freedom. She finishes by saying, "Will you now, when you are needed most, stop at only words? Is that the sort of men you are? I ask only that you act upon the beliefs of which you have so strongly spoken, and in which you so strongly believe."

It is very fitting that this scene takes place in a church, because all too often that is true of the church. We talk a good game, know the right things to say, can pray nice-sounding prayers, and even quote scripture. Yet all too often we stop at only words.

We live in a world that needs God. There are people all around who are lost, searching for some meaning and purpose, looking for answers, and wanting to feel like they have worth and are loved. And too often they don't find what they need, get the answers they want, or feel loved at all.

Jesus' teaching in the New Testament requires action. It is impossible to put his teachings and commands into practice while doing nothing. Jesus' teachings, God's commands, call us to live out what we say and show others what we know by our actions, not just our words.

Matthew 28:19–20 says, "Therefore go and make disciples of all nations, baptizing them in the name of the Father and the Son and the Holy Spirit, and teaching them all I have commanded you. And surely I am with you always, to the very end of the age" (NIV).

The two key points in these verses are as follows:
1. The command we are given

2. The last sentence spoken

Allow me to explain each of these points briefly.

Firstly, the last command Jesus gives us before he returns to heaven is to go and share Jesus with the world. *Go*, a verb, implies action. It's a command to do something, not sit and wait for something to happen. Jesus tells us to get up, go out of our doors, and meet the world where they are. To take initiative and be active in sharing Jesus with others, both through our words and through our actions. To go into a lost and dying world and share with them the good news of Jesus. To go and make disciples of Jesus.

Secondly, the last sentence of this final command is an encouragement: "And surely I am with you always, to the very end of the age." Why does Jesus need to say this? He is encouraging us because we are to engage the world. Remember the command before that encouragement is a call to action, a command to go. Action can be hard, uncomfortable, challenging, and can even bring pain. So we need to be encouraged that through it all, Jesus is right there with us.

Every follower of Christ has been commanded to do, go, engage, initiate, and be active in sharing Jesus with the world. It is this very command that should be the passion of every follower of Christ and the vision and purpose of every church. And the way we go about obeying this command is much simpler than we have made it.

When Jesus was asked what the two most important commands were, he answered, "Love the Lord your God with all your heart and with all your soul and with all your mind. This is the first and greatest commandment. And the second is like it: Love your neighbor as yourself. All the Law and the Prophets hang on these two commandments "(Matthew 22:37–40, NIV).

Earlier, I said that Jesus came to show us how to live out what the Law and prophets said in the Old Testament. In this passage, he simplifies the lifestyle of a follower of Christ into one word: love. When we love others, we are actually show them Christ. In 1 John, chapter four, it says twice that "God is love."

So often we as followers of Christ think it comes down to having great programs in the church, putting on big events, hearing amazing speakers, and doing exciting advertising in order to reach the world for Christ. However, when we see how Jesus did it and taught us to do it, we see that what really attracts people is our love for them—no matter how difficult that love is. Programs, events, amazing speakers, and exciting advertising are all great, but without love, they are what 1 Corinthians 13 refers to as a noisy gong or clanging cymbal.

In John 13:34–35, Jesus says to his disciples, "A new command I give you: Love one another. As I have loved you, so you must love one another. By this all men will know that you are my disciples, if you love one another" (NIV). The new command is not that we should love others; that command has been around for a long time. The new command is that we are to love others the way Jesus loved us. We know how Jesus loved us; he sacrificed everything to die for us. We are in turn to sacrifice everything for the sake of others.

In fact, according to Jesus in the verses above, the world will know we are followers of Christ by our love, not by our words, programs, events, buildings, or anything else we as the church often like to do to reach the world.

In fact, love is so essential to being a follower of Christ that 1 John 4:20–21 says, "If anyone says, 'I love God,' yet hates his brother, he is a liar. For anyone who does not love his brother, whom he has seen, cannot love God, whom he has not seen. And he has given us this command: Whoever loves God must also love his brother" (NIV). If we don't love those around us, then we don't love God. To love God means that we love others.

Jesus came to teach us to love others, to put others before ourselves, to think of others' needs first, and to care for those who need care. As followers of Christ, our job is simple: love the world straight to Jesus. That is what being a follower of Christ is all about. Everything else is secondary.

Second Misconception: Being a Christian Means Saying a Prayer

I've yet to find in the Bible a reference to someone closing their eyes, raising their hands, and saying a prayer asking Jesus into their heart, but that is what many churches have come to teach. We give invitations at the end of a church service or at an event, saying things like "no one is looking, so if you want to accept Jesus into your heart please raise your hand and repeat this prayer."

When I look at Scripture, I see verses like Romans 10:9–10, which says, "That if you confess with your mouth Jesus as Lord, and believe in your heart that God raised Him from the dead, you shall be saved; for with the heart man believes, resulting in righteousness, and with the mouth he confesses, resulting in salvation" (NASB), or Acts 16:30–31, which says, "'Sirs, what must I do to be saved?' And they said, 'Believe in the Lord Jesus, and you shall be saved, you and your household'"(NASB).

I didn't see a single reference to closing your eyes, raising your hands, and saying some pretty prayer to ask Jesus into your heart. What I did see was that it rests on our belief that Jesus is Lord and our confession of that belief out loud with our mouth.

Raising your hand or saying a prayer to accept Christ is not necessarily a bad idea. It can actually be a great way for our minds to have that beginning point, since we think about things on a timeline. Plus, prayer is how we speak to God, and to ask him for forgiveness for our sins requires that we talk to him. So raising a hand and saying a prayer isn't necessarily wrong. But, the problem is that it has become popular to believe that if you raise your hand and say a prayer, that's all there is to it.

Now don't misunderstand me here. I totally believe what Ephesians 2:8–9 tells us: "For by grace you have been saved through faith; and that not of yourselves, it is the gift of God; not as a result of works, that no one should boast" (NASB). Salvation is a gift that is given to us, and we can't earn it at all by anything that we do. I completely believe that. My concern is that we have stopped at saying a prayer or raising our hands, and therefore we've neglected the complete truth of salvation. I fear we've made it simply a moment in our life, rather than a commitment that defines our life.

Philippians 2:12 talks about "continuing to work out our salvation with fear and trembling." James 2:26 says, "As the body without the spirit is dead, so faith without works is dead" (NIV).

What we need to understand is that salvation is not just a point in time (though yes, there is that beginning point when we give our lives to Christ), but also a lifestyle that comes from the choice to follow Christ. It is a lifestyle that should bear fruit, a lifestyle where we are continually being worked on and perfected, a lifestyle where we are striving to be holy just as God is holy, and a lifestyle that those around us should see.

And that choice is not to be made because no one is looking so that we can raise our hand in secret. Rather, it is to be made out loud in front of others so that everyone knows. The problem with making it too easy to accept Christ is that we lose the aspect of a lifestyle commitment of following Christ, and that has hurt true Christianity. Too often people raise their hands because no one is looking and because that is the easy thing to do, but they aren't really completely committed to Christ. If you want to know if people really mean it, have them do it in front of other people.

What I have begun doing is this. When I give the gospel and an invitation in youth group, I tell the students that if they want to talk more about following Christ, then they should stick around as everyone else leaves, and we'll talk. Sometimes part of the invitation will include having them raise their hands, but I don't just leave it with that. I will then dismiss youth group a little early, and all those who want to talk more can stay while the rest leave. That lets me know they are serious, because it is no secret that they are staying to talk to me or what the subject matter is. It is out there in the open for all to see. And isn't that the point?

Jesus didn't live his life quietly but was very vocal that God was his father and that we are to love other people. He didn't tell those he had chosen to spread his word, his disciples, to do so in secret. Look at the disciples and how they lived their lives: all of them lived out loud in front of everyone with no shame of what they believed. All of them except John (I'm not counting Judas at this point) even died horrible deaths for living that way.

We do a huge injustice to Christ and those seeking to follow him when we make being a follower of Christ something that begins in secret and is little more than a prayer. It's time we understood that living for Christ requires us to stand up and be seen, that we will be working out our salvation until the day Christ comes back because we are imperfect and still struggle with sin, and that following Christ requires a huge commitment.

Christianity is not a religion; it is a way of life. Being a follower of Christ does not mean saying a prayer or raising your hand in secret, but rather it is the choice to follow Christ and the lifestyle that goes along with it.

Worship

W*orship* is a word that gets tossed around a lot in the church. In fact, I bet you hear that word at least once every time you go to a church service. It is a very popular word, and rightly so. Worship is an important and foundational concept when it comes to truly living a life of following Christ.

Often, this word will be used when talking about the time in a church service when the congregation gathers to sing songs corporately. Many refer to this time as "the time of worship." Others use the word to refer to a kind of music. I've heard people say, "I can't worship to this style of music" or "that is my favorite style of worship." Still others simply refer to the whole Sunday morning service as the "worship service."

The problem is that this is the incorrect usage. It is incorrect because it doesn't fit with the true meaning of the word, and it is incorrect because it limits the power of the word. Worship is far beyond a church service or a style of music.

To fully understand the depth of the word *worship*, we need to first look at the real meaning of the word.

Our word *worship* comes from two words: the word *worth* and the suffix *-ship*.

The definition of *worth* is "the value of something measured by its qualities or by the esteem in which it is held" (merriam-webster.

com/dictionary). The more esteem we give to something, the more value it has—which determines its amount of *worth*.

-ship is a suffix that you place at the end of a word to denote condition. For example, the word *friend*, with the suffix *-ship*, becomes *friendship*. Friend is a general word; *-ship* makes it personal because it makes the word *friend* a condition, not just a word. *Friendship* is the word *friend* being applied on a personal level.

Now add the two words *worth* and *-ship* together, and you get *worth-ship*, or *worship*. The definition of *worship* is "to be devoted to, full of admiration for, and to have or express feelings of profound adoration for a person or object" (dictionary.com).

When we put it all together, *worship* is the declaration of how much we value, admire, and are devoted to someone or something. Whatever we place a high value on, admire, and are devoted to is what we *worship*.

Now that we know what the word really means, the second thing we need to understand is the fact that we are all worshippers. Every single one of us worships someone or something. It is our nature as humans to assign a value and worth to someone or something, thus worshipping that to which we've assigned the value and worth. There are certain people we hold in high regard, certain activities that are very important to us, and certain valuables that to us are just that—valuable. In the purest sense of the word, anything that has greatest value to us is something we will worship.

I know that it can seem weird thinking about worship in this sense, but that is what happens when we have used the word in the wrong way for so many years. After a while, the truth is harder to accept because we are used to our perspectives. It is time we saw the truth for what it is.

No one wastes time and energy showing love, admiration, or devotion to something or someone he or she doesn't care about. It has to have value to us before we make it have worth in our eyes and our actions.

One way to know what has value and worth to you is to look at what you spend the majority of your "choice time" on. What I mean by "choice time" is the time in your life that you can choose how to spend. That doesn't include the hours you spend going to school or the hours you are required to work. What it does include is the time you have after you've finished your expected amount of work, when school or work is over, and you actually have the choice of what to do.

You show me how you spend the majority of your choice time, and I'll show you what you love, admire, and are devoted to. And by definition, what you love, admire, and are devoted to is what you place worth and value on, which is what you worship.

Some of you might worship work because you choose to do extra work with the majority of your choice time; some of you might worship video games; some of you might worship going to the gym; etc.

Is doing extra work, playing video games, or going to the gym wrong? No, not in and of themselves. But when they or anything else become a priority that you place over your personal relationship with Jesus and serving him, then they become wrong. Anything that distracts you from God himself is wrong.

So, how do we worship God in the true sense of the word? How can we as followers of Christ live in such a way that we place worth and value on loving, admiring, and being devoted to God?

Matthew 22:37 tells us to "Love the Lord your God with all your heart and with all your soul and with all your mind" (NIV). To worship God we must first love him with everything that we are. We have to make him top priority in our hearts, in our souls, and in our minds. If you can find an area of your life that is not affected by one of those three areas, then you can do with that area whatever you want. (I hope you are noticing the sarcasm here!)

The truth is, those three areas cover every inch of who we are and every inch of our lives. We are to love God with everything that we are. That begins with us placing on him top value and worth in our lives, which then gives way to us admiring him and being devoted to him. That is how we worship him.

Romans 12:1 says, "Therefore, I urge you, brothers, in view of God's mercy, to offer your bodies as living sacrifices, holy and pleasing to God—this is your spiritual act of worship" (NIV). Paul in this passage lets us know what we need to do to worship God:

offer our bodies as living sacrifices that are holy and pleasing to him. "Our bodies" refers to our lives—who we are physically, emotionally, and spiritually. The giving of our entire lives to God is the act of worshipping him.

Anyone who knows me can tell you that doing missions is very important to me. Whether it's going to the local rescue mission in town to feed the homeless, working at a food bank, or going on a trip, I place high importance on doing mission projects both here and abroad. The reason it is so important to me is because it is so important to God. Throughout Scripture we are commanded to help the poor, take care of the sick, and spread the Word of God to everyone.

In my ministry I try to make sure we do a minimum of five local service projects a year, and then I always have a big summer mission project as well. What has always been interesting to me—and has bothered me as well—is that whenever I introduce either a service project that we will be doing on a Saturday or a mission trip that will be a week or two long, I initially get a lot of response from people that they are interested in going. I hear things like "That sounds like a great experience" or "I'd like to be a part of that" or "What a great thing to do!"

Yet, despite all the positive feedback I initially get, several of those who seemed interested in the beginning end up dropping off when it is comes time to commit, especially when it comes to a trip that is a week or two long. And those who initially expressed interest always have a reason why they decided not to go. They have a family trip to take, they will probably need to use that time to get extra work done, they can't afford to be gone for a week, or they don't have the money necessary to go.

Remember what worship is: placing value and worth on something we love, admire, and are devoted to. Romans 12:1 told us that to worship God requires us to be a living sacrifice. Being a living sacrifice requires that while we are alive we make sacrifices to serve God, and we make these sacrifices to serve God because we love, admire, and are devoted to him.

Worship is a verb, an action, something we do. When we obey God's commands, we show both him and the world that we place value and worth on God and his Word, which is an act of worship. When we serve other people out of love for them and God, we are worshipping God. When we give our time or money to the church or an organization dedicated to serving God, we are worshipping God. When we give up something that we wanted to do in order to do something God has commanded us to do, even if it is uncomfortable, we are worshipping God.

Until we ascribe the condition of value to God through our love, admiration, and devotion, we can never truly offer our lives as living sacrifices to God. And if we never truly offer our lives as living sacrifices to God, then we can never fully live for him. God is an all-or-nothing kind of God; 90 percent doesn't cut it.

Matthew 6:21 tells us that where our treasure is shows where our heart is. In other words, you will devote your heart to what you care about.

Worship is not a time of the service and it is not a style of music; it is an attitude and condition of your heart. Worship is an action and a lifestyle. Do you love, admire, and feel devotion toward God, or don't you? You can truly be in the right attitude and mind-set to worship God when you are at work or at home. On the flip side, you can be in a church service singing all your favorite songs and never even come close to actually worshiping God.

Worship begins in our hearts, not in our church service. It plays itself out in our daily lives, not while we sit in our favorite pew. It is an action that shows both God and others that Jesus is the Lord of our lives, which can happen no matter where we are or what we are doing.

Treasures

My first full-time youth pastor job was at a church in Omaha, Nebraska. Every year at that church we would have a big business meeting to discuss the ministry of the church and vote on the budget for the upcoming year.

In one such meeting the church's treasurer stood up and informed everyone that we might have to start dipping into a special savings account the church had. This particular savings account wasn't normally touched, so the possibility of using it got people talking immediately, which led to more people talking. In fact, it got to the point where the discussion was beginning to get heated, so the senior pastor had everyone take a break to cool down before we continued the discussion.

A couple days before this meeting I had taken my youth group down to a local homeless shelter to do volunteer work. We had spent several hours there sorting through donated items that were given to those who are homeless and less fortunate. As we discussed our "financial troubles," I began to think about that experience, and it began to really bother me.

We as followers of Christ here in America have bought into the whole "American Dream" idea of having enough money plus extra saved in case something happens. And while being smart with money is very important, we've lost the need to trust in God because we have such overabundance in this country.

A few days after that meeting I shared in a lesson how we saw the people at that homeless shelter as not having what they need to survive. But in all honesty, that wasn't true at all. Yes, they had much less than we do, and we should help them. But they had a place to stay and food to eat for that day—and isn't that the practical definition of a need? To be completely blunt, we don't need anything more than what is necessary for surviving today. Everything else is extra.

Exodus 16:4–5 and 13–21 says,

> Then the Lord said to Moses, "I will rain down bread from heaven for you. The people are to go out each day and gather enough for that day. In this way I will test them and see whether they will follow my instructions. On the sixth day they are to prepare what they bring in, and that is to be twice as much as they gather on the other days. ...That evening quail came and covered the camp, and in the morning there was a layer of dew around the camp. When the dew was gone, thin flakes like frost on the ground appeared on the desert floor. When the Israelites saw it, they said to each other, "What is it?" For they did not know what it was. Moses said to them, "It is the bread the Lord has given you to eat. This is what the Lord has commanded: 'Each one is to gather as much as he needs. Take an omer for each person you have in your tent.'" The Israelites did as they were told; some gathered much, some little. And when they measured it by the omer, he who gathered much did not have too much, and he who gathered little did not have too little. Each one gathered as much as he needed. Then Moses said to them, "No one is to keep any of it until morning." However, some of them paid no attention to Moses; they kept part of it until morning, but it was full of maggots and began to smell. So Moses was angry

with them. Each morning everyone gathered as much as he needed, and when the sun grew hot, it melted away. (NIV)

Israel is wandering around the desert and will be at it for a while (that's putting it lightly), and in this passage we see how God took care of their need for food. It must have been weird to have food show up outside their tents like that. And while we often focus on the fact that God provides in this passage, which is true, we often miss another very important part of that provision.

God told the people of Israel that they were only to take enough for that day; none of them were to keep any of it until morning. But some people didn't listen and took extra. And look at what happened to the extra that they took—it went bad and became unusable.

Now, using my human and American perspectives, I would say that it was smart for them to take more than what they needed for that day, because what if it doesn't come tomorrow? We need to take care of ourselves and our families by making sure we have food, so taking extra to save for the next day is smart, at least from a worldly perspective.

So why would God command them not to take extra? Was he trying to be cruel to them by making them worry about whether it would come again the next day? No, he was in fact teaching them a very important lesson: to trust in God for your needs instead of yourself. The Israelites had to have complete trust in God, because they were only given enough for that day. They would have to wait till tomorrow to find out if God would provide for them again.

Jesus did some teaching about this same lesson in Matthew 6:25–34 when he says,

> Therefore I tell you, do not worry about your life, what you will eat or drink; or about your body, what you will wear. Is not life more important than food, and the body more important than clothes? Look at the birds of the air; they do not sow or reap or store away in barns, and yet your heavenly Father feeds them. Are you not much more valuable than they?

Who of you by worrying can add a single hour to his life? And why do you worry about clothes? See how the lilies of the field grow. They do not labor or spin. Yet I tell you that not even Solomon in all his splendor was dressed like one of these. If that is how God clothes the grass of the field, which is here today and tomorrow is thrown into the fire, will he not much more clothe you, O you of little faith? So do not worry, saying, 'What shall we eat?' or 'What shall we drink?' or 'What shall we wear?' For the pagans run after all these things, and your heavenly Father knows that you need them. But seek first his kingdom and his righteousness, and all these things will be given to you as well. Therefore do not worry about tomorrow, for tomorrow will worry about itself. Each day has enough trouble of its own. (NIV)

We as followers of Christ should never ever worry about anything we need, because God will take care of us. Jesus even said we shouldn't even worry about anything for tomorrow because today has enough to take care of.

We live in a country—and world—that makes materialism a top priority in life. We always have to have bigger, better, more, newer, nicer. We have the mentality that we need these things, that they are essential and important. We have to have a savings account, brand new cars, a big house, regular vacations, the newest version of technology, and everything else we want and desire. We confuse want and desire with need and necessity.

The problem is that we have so much excess in America that we could go months without having to trust God for our food, clothing, money, etc. When that becomes what we think we deserve, we stop looking to God to provide our every need, and we begin to look to ourselves and our stuff to take care of us. We place our trust and faith in ourselves and our possessions and not in the one who gave us everything we have.

In the summer of 2008, I led a mission trip to Puerto Vallarta, Mexico. One of the hardest things we did while we were down there was to take food and other essential items to give out to people who lived at the city dump. That's right—they lived at it. On one side of the street was the city dump, complete with vultures circling it. On the other side of the street were houses, all of them made out of the trash they had pulled out of that dump.

We saw people actually in the city dump looking for things they could use. I saw a little girl, probably no more than six, pulling a baby stroller and collecting strips of metal. Some kids were running around with no clothes on, others with clothes that were filthy and way too small.

While we were there passing out these items and sharing the gospel we met an older lady. We learned that she had lived there her whole life. Her kids were born there, as well as her grandkids. She had never once left the city dump; it was literally her life.

This old lady didn't know what a Wal-Mart was. She had never gone on an expensive vacation to another country just for the fun of it. She didn't go to Sam's Club or Costco to buy food in bulk. She didn't own a car, let alone two or three cars. She spent the majority of her life living day to day, hoping to have enough food and other essentials just for that day. She had a much better understanding of the difference between a need and a want.

For Americans, it is easy to get comfortable with how things have been. We've been a comfortable and secure country for a long time, and that has caused us to get used to being like that. What is dangerous is that when things change and make us even a little uncomfortable we lose our cool and become all worried—which shows that we've placed our trust in our comfort and money and the whole "American Dream."

As followers of Christ, we are supposed to live as though this world is not our home; we are simply passing through on our way to heaven. Yet we have all too often taken on the ways of America and the world and have forgotten the ways of Jesus. We have made this world our home. We have placed our trust in our comfort and money and the whole "American Dream."

As followers of Christ, we are supposed to do just that: follow Christ. Christ never preached being comfortable and secure and having everything we want, and he never said we needed more than our daily bread. He preached unconditionally loving everyone, praying for your enemies, blessing those who persecute you, taking care of the poor and needy, telling those around us of his great love for us, being holy just like he is, and trusting him and him alone.

What is sad is that 99 percent of those who claim to be followers of Christ would read this and agree with every word—but then would continue to live with their trust in their comfort and money and the whole "American Dream." Knowledge does not mean we obey; it just means we know. To obey is an action that we have to do intentionally, like trusting in God instead of our resources.

Luke 18:18 and 20–25 says,

> A certain ruler asked him, "Good teacher, what must I do to inherit eternal life?"…"You know the commandments: 'Do not commit adultery, do not murder, do not steal, do not give false testimony, honor your father and mother.'" "All these I have kept since I was a boy," he said. When Jesus heard this, he said to him, "You still lack one thing. Sell everything you have and give to the poor, and you will have treasure in heaven. Then come, follow me." When he heard this, he became very sad, because he was a man of great wealth. Jesus looked at him and said, "How hard it is for the rich to enter the kingdom of God! Indeed, it is easier for a camel to go through the eye of a needle than for a rich man to enter the kingdom of God." (NIV)

That last statement spoken by Jesus is a very hard statement—hard but true. Just look at our country right now. There is a serious epidemic happening where people don't think they need God because they have stuff. When we have all the stuff we want, why would we ever need to trust in God?

That passage in Luke shows us that God wants us to give what we have to those who need it more so we don't begin to trust in our things instead of in him. It also proves by the reaction of the man that the more we have, the harder it is to give it away, because we begin to trust in stuff instead of God. It is a vicious cycle that is very hard to break.

Matthew 6:19–21 tells us, "Do not lay up for yourselves treasures upon earth, where moth and rust destroy, and where thieves break in and steal. But lay up for yourselves treasures in heaven, where neither moth nor rust destroys, and where thieves do not break in or steal; for where your treasure is, there will your heart be also" (NASB).

It is not just a nice suggestion that Jesus makes. It is a command. It says, "Do not lay up for yourselves treasures upon earth." But we often change it to say "make sure not to lay up too many treasures for yourselves upon the earth, but at the same time lay up enough treasures that you'll be comfortable and not be in need."

Look at where you spend the majority of your resources. This will tell you what you love and admire, to what you are devoted, or upon what you place value. As we learned in the last chapter, that is what you worship. So the real question is this: do you worship God or money? The Bible says in Matthew 6:24 that you can't serve both; it is one or the other.

Having new cars, savings accounts, the ability to go on vacations, etc., are not bad things. The problem, however, is when we see them as needs instead of blessings from God. When God blesses us, we should be thankful for it and be willing to allow God to bless others, through our generosity, with what God has blessed us with. We should, according to what Jesus told the rich young ruler in Luke 18, be using what we have to help others rather than ourselves.

I had the privilege of going to Haiti shortly after the earthquake of January 2010 to do some relief work. While there I spoke with a couple different church leaders in the area. When I heard what they said, I was both amazed and ashamed at the same time. They both said to me, "We never had much, and what we did have was taken from us in the earthquake. But we have Christ, and that is all we really need, anyway. Christ is enough."

I was amazed at what a godly perspective they had after such a major tragedy, and I was ashamed of how often I trust in my stuff rather than in God alone.

May we as followers of Christ trust in God and not our money; may we serve God and not ourselves or our stuff. May we have the perspective that God is enough, and that everything else is just extra blessings from him that we can turn around and bless others with.

Faith

I shared in a previous chapter that I had led a mission trip to Puerto Vallarta, Mexico in 2008. I knew someone who owned a condo and had ties to a ministry there. So we after we worked out the details, I began to plan our trip.

When I announced this trip there was a lot of interest. In fact, I had so many students and adults signing up to go that we had to put a cap on the amount of people we would take because the condo only fit so many. When the deadline to sign up came, we had nineteen people going! This was the biggest mission team I had ever led to date, and it was awesome to see the excitement about this trip as well as the commitment to it.

Then came the fundraising. I announced to the church on the first Sunday of March 2008 that the estimated total cost of this trip would be sixteen thousand dollars. The trip was scheduled for the first week of July 2008, which meant we had three months to raise the money. It was then that the doubts and fears of this commitment came out. I had people tell me that they didn't see us raising that amount in such a short period of time. Others wondered whether I had gotten in over my head allowing so many to come. I began to look at the numbers and costs over and over, and I even started to question if this was going to work.

Ten weeks later, on May 4, 2008, I stood before the church and reported that not only had the full amount been raised, but we had gone over our needed amount by a thousand dollars!

Philippians 4:19 says, "And my God shall supply all your needs according to His riches in glory in Christ Jesus" (NASB). The question isn't "Will God provide?"; the question is "Will we as his followers believe that he will provide?"

Faith is both completely essential in the life of a follower of Christ and one of the hardest parts of being a follower of Christ. Let's be honest for a minute. Following someone we've never seen is not easy. Sometimes we wish that we could just see God for a moment; then having faith in him would be so much easier. Yet if we did see him, that would go against the very idea of having faith.

Hebrews 11:1 defines faith for us: "Now faith is being sure of what we hope for and certain of what we do not see" (NIV). The phrases "what we hope for" and "what we do not see" both refer to that which we can't control and can't see at this point in time. Simply put, faith only happens if we trust in God when we can't see him or what is to come. If we saw him or knew the future, there wouldn't be a need for faith.

Each of us has a choice in life: the choice between trusting and placing our faith in ourselves or trusting and placing our faith in God. I have never understood why a human, who is imperfect, would want to trust him- or herself. This doesn't happen with anything else. If anything else was known to be prone to failing, we would never trust it—yet we do that very thing with ourselves.

Several years ago I was having a conversation with a student who was having a real issue in her life. The youth group was on a camping trip, and this girl and I were sitting at the picnic table talking while everyone else was making s'mores. As we talked she shared her life story with me.

This girl came from a broken home. From what I could tell, her mom was not around, and she "lived" with her dad. I put *lived* in quotation marks because it might be debatable based on the conditions of this living arrangement. Her dad was a drug addict who would smoke pot—and let her smoke pot with him! Not only that, her dad would let her stay with guys whenever she wanted. This girl was fourteen or fifteen years old, and she was living with a drug addict dad who let her sleep around.

As she was sharing all this with me, she told me, and I quote, "I personally don't believe in hell. But if hell did exist, it would be my life." That is how this girl felt about her life—that it was literally hell.

I saw this as my opportunity to share with her about the love of Jesus. I began to share how Jesus can give us peace in the midst of a life of turmoil, about how Jesus loves us no matter what, and that giving our lives to Jesus can give us meaning and purpose for our lives.

I'll never forget her response. She looked me straight in the eyes and said, "I can't give control of my life to someone else. My life is hell, but at least I am the one in control."

While this is a sad story, her response demonstrates a very important point. Faith comes down to who is in control. Who we want to be in control of our lives will determine in whom we place our faith. We fear giving control of our lives to someone else, so we hold onto that control and place our faith in ourselves. We fear giving up control of our lives because we don't want to trust anyone.

Yet if any of us are at all honest with ourselves, no one has the ability to say that he or she is in complete control of their lives. In fact, we have little to no control at all.

Think about it. You are alive right now because your body is breathing in oxygen, oxygen that you didn't create and over which you have no control. You, right now, have a pulse, showing you that your heart is beating and distributing blood to the rest of your body. If your heart decides to stop working, you can't control that. Now, you can control some of the circumstances around you to help make sure your heart stays healthy enough to beat and distribute blood, but that is at best indirect control. And no matter how much indirect control you exercise, your heart is ultimately still in control, because if it stops, then it stops.

And even if we do our absolute best with the amount of indirect control we have, there are so many variables outside of our realm of control. This life is full of so many things that happen to us over which we have no control, no matter how much we try. We are at the mercy of the environment around us.

True faith only happens when we can realize and admit that we are not in control, and in turn give it to the one who is in control: the creator and sustainer of the world, God.

We can say we believe in God, but that isn't faith. Saying the words and even knowing the truth is not the same as putting faith in that truth and living according to the truth. In James 2:19, it says, "You believe that there is one God. Good! Even the demons believe that—and shudder" (NIV).

My first two years of college I was part of the soccer team. I was not very good—in fact, I was by all accounts bad. But since it was a small college and the players needed enough people to man a team, I volunteered. I had played football since junior high, was somewhat athletic, and knew how to run, so I gave it a shot.

My sophomore year we had a tournament in Dallas, Texas, that was going to take the whole weekend. It was during a time that had been very difficult for me. Growing up, I had always done well in school, but the reality of college being tougher than high school was setting in, and I was struggling in some of my classes. In addition to playing soccer and going to school, I had a full-time job because I needed to pay for school, my car, food, and other essentials—including dates, since I had a girlfriend at the time. I also was volunteering at a church as a leader in the youth group, and I've always been one to dive into whatever I do 100 percent. Through all of this, I was starting to crack under the pressure.

So I was really looking forward to getting away for a weekend, to just get away from my life for a few days and recharge. Since we were in Omaha and the tournament was in Dallas, we were leaving at 4:00 a.m. I packed the night before, set my alarm for 3:30 a.m., and then went to bed. At 3:30 a.m. my alarm went off, and I jumped out of bed. I got dressed, made sure I had everything I would need, and then checked outside to see if the van was there. It was still fifteen or twenty minutes before 4:00 a.m. and the van was not there yet, so I sat down on my couch to wait.

The next thing I knew, I was waking up on my couch at 8:00 a.m.! As soon as I realized what time it was, I jumped up and ran outside, but of course the van was gone. I was so upset that I missed the van, and I had so much pent-up stress and anger from that semester that I began to unpack my clothes by throwing things everywhere.

As I was angrily unpacking, my phone rang. It was my coach. He said to me, "Hey, Woogy, we stopped for gas in Kansas and realized that you weren't here." All I could say at the time was "yeah." He then proceeded to tell me what hotel we were staying at and told me to drive down and meet the team there.

So I switched my car for my girlfriend's, because hers could handle a long distance trip much better than mine, I repacked my stuff, and I started my drive to Dallas. It is a ten-hour drive from Omaha, which is a long time to be by yourself when you are stressed and angry.

After passing through Oklahoma City, there was a stretch of nothing where I couldn't even pick up a radio station. So I was sitting there, in silence, driving and stewing. The frustrations and stresses of the past few months were running over and over in my head, and I had such a hard time not losing control of my anger at that point. Have you ever been so mad that you begin to breathe faster and harder, and it feels like your heart is beating harder? Well, that was me at that point.

As I drove in silence and thought about all this, a verse popped into my head and kept repeating over and over and over. I could see it in my mind's eye; I could hear it in my head, over and over and over. It was a verse that I had known for a long time, and it was like this verse was beating me on the head to get my attention.

The more I heard this verse, the more I began to calm down and think about it. After a while I said, "Okay, God, what are you trying to show me?" The verse was Psalms 46:10, which says, "Cease striving and know that I am God; I will be exalted among the nations, I will be exalted in the earth"(NASB).

I had spent the past several months doing everything I could to fix and handle the situations in my life. I had been relying on my own strength to get through life, and I was at the end of my rope because of it.

What I needed to remember, and what God was showing me by constantly reminding me of that verse, is that I am not God—but he is! I was not created to handle everything this life throws at me, so I needed to stop trying. I needed to let the Creator, the one who was capable of handling everything, have control in my life. God wanted me to trust him, have faith in him, and lean on him.

That was, and still is, one of the most painful lessons I've ever had to learn. It took me a while to be able to trust in God completely with my life. After all, I am human and want to be in control of it myself. And it is still a regular struggle in my life to continue to allow him to be in complete control.

About a month or so after that trip I was sitting in chapel singing praise songs, and I came to the point where I just broke down. I had been standing, and I had to sit down because I was crying so hard. I was finally at the place where I was tired of trying and willing to give it all to God, because I just couldn't take it anymore. After I had finished crying I looked up, lifted my hand into the air, and opened it up as a symbol that I was giving it to God.

The moment I opened my hand and gave it to God, I felt one hundred pounds lighter! I suddenly had joy and peace. I was, for the first time in a very long time, willing to have complete faith in God. I was giving him control of my life, and for once I understood what it meant to fully trust him.

Proverbs 3:5–6 says, "Trust in the Lord with all your heart and lean not on your own understanding. In all your ways acknowledge him and he will make your paths straight" (NIV). Verse five tells us to not lean on our own understanding, but to trust in God. When we trust in ourselves we are leaning on our own understanding of the situation and not trusting in God like the verse tells us to.

Faith is an action that we have to do, not a word that we say. We need to place our trust in God for every aspect of our lives, not just certain ones. If you're holding onto anything, you aren't fully trusting God, and your faith is incomplete. Faith is more than knowing about God and believing in him; it is the act of placing your entire life in his hands and then removing yours.

There is an amusement park a few hours south of Omaha in Kansas City. At this amusement park, there is a ride called the Rip Cord. This is a ride where you are strapped into a harness, and the harness is attached to a three cords, each one attached to a different pole. Once you are fully strapped in, the ride begins to haul you up to the top of one of the poles, which is about two hundred feet high. Once you've reached the top, you pull a handle that releases you from the cord attached to that pole, and you immediately free-fall for several seconds. Eventually the two other cords attached to two other poles become straight and tight, and you swing back and forth.

I have a fear of heights—which is really a fear of going *splat*. If I fell slowly and landed softly, I wouldn't be afraid of heights. It's the splat that happens at the bottom that causes me to be afraid of heights. So to me, this ride is insane, and I will never do it!

Now, I'd watched countless people do this ride, and I'd never once seen it malfunction. This ride is very popular and runs all season, and I'd never heard of it breaking and killing someone. Every year I took my youth group to this park, and every year I had several students who would go on this ride—and nothing bad ever happened.

Yet no matter how much knowledge I had about that ride, no matter how safe it proved itself to be, no matter how much I saw it work, I was not willing to do it myself. I was not willing to put my faith in it, to trust my life to that harness.

Faith is not the knowledge of God. Faith is the act of strapping yourself in and putting your life in his hands. Faith is trusting in God and not yourself.

Spiritual Warfare

When I was in high school, my youth group put on a weekend outreach event one year. For this event we brought in a special speaker, and we also had a praise band. I was up onstage helping lead one of the times of praise (I am a terrible singer but very energetic, so the organizers unplugged my microphone and simply had me up there for my energy). As we were singing, I noticed that a student in front of me was starting to look pale. As we continued to sing, he continued to get paler and paler until he looked like a clean sheet of white paper.

This student eventually was so sick that he ended up having the leave the room. He went into my dad's office to lie down (my dad was the senior pastor). A few minutes later, my dad came back and had my youth pastor and the special speaker leave with him.

It was at this point that a weird feeling started to fill the room. And I wasn't the only one to notice it, either; the whole room could sense it, so much so that the band actually stopped playing. The leader of the band had everyone begin to pray, because we could sense that something was going on. A little while later, the student emerged from my dad's office, looking like he hadn't slept in a few days.

The reason this student had become so sick was that he had been possessed by a demon. My dad, my youth pastor, and the speaker had been in the office for a while actually speaking to the demon that possessed this kid.

When most people in the church think of spiritual warfare, that kind of story is what they think about. And while that is correct, the truth is that that is a very limited part of it. Spiritual warfare is much deeper and broader than that. It is so much deeper, in fact, that demon possession is actually more of an outcome or effect of what spiritual warfare really is.

Spiritual warfare is really an all-inclusive battle that involves everything in our lives. Sound a little extreme? Let me explain.

Genesis 1:27 says, "So God created man in his own image, in the image of God he created him; male and female he created them" (NIV). We are created in the image of God, each and every one of us. That means that we all have a spiritual side to us. That spiritual side is often referred to as our soul, or our spirit. That is the part of us that will continue on in eternity after our physical bodies are gone.

It is that very soul that God and Satan are battling over. God loves us and wants us to be in relationship with him so that our souls may spend eternity in heaven. Satan, on the other hand, hates us and wants to keep us from giving our lives to God so that we may spend eternity in hell with him. This war does not happen in the physical realm (although we do see and feel the effects of the battle in the physical realm), but rather it is in the spiritual realm that God and Satan exist. And because we have a spiritual side to us via our souls, we are also connected to that spiritual realm; many just don't realize it because they have never become aware of it.

In Ephesians 6:12, it says, "For our struggle is not against flesh and blood, but against the rulers, against the powers, against the world forces of this darkness, against the spiritual forces of wickedness in the heavenly places" (NASB). It says that this struggle is our struggle, not just God's. We are a part of this battle against "the powers, against the world forces of darkness, against the spiritual forces of wickedness in the heavenly places."

Once we realize that we are a part of this spiritual battle, the next step is to understand how the battle plays out. The best way to do that is to learn our enemy and his strategy.

1 Peter 5:8 tells us that "your enemy the devil prowls around like a roaring lion looking for someone to devour" (NIV). John 8:44 says, "He was a murderer from the beginning, not holding to the truth, for there is no truth in him. When he lies, he speaks his native language, for he is a liar and the father of lies" (NIV).

Satan's strategy in this spiritual battle is to lie to and deceive us in order to keep us from giving our lives to God. All he cares about is devouring us, and he uses his lies and deception to do just that. Satan will do anything to keep us deceived so that we can't see the truth. And he will use anything in our lives that he can deceive us with in order to accomplish that goal. Anything that he can use as a foothold in our life that will keep us from focusing on God is the way Satan fights against us and God in this spiritual battle.

Everyone struggles with different things, but we all struggle. Satan will use those struggles against us, and he will work to keep us so caught up in our own struggle that we either forget the truth of God's forgiveness and grace or never see it in the first place. He will try to convince us that being as busy as possible is good, and when we are too busy doing stuff, we are too busy to give time to learn about and listen to God. He will cause things to happen in our lives that can make us depressed or sad, angry or hateful. He will lure us into focusing on making more money or being in relationships instead of focusing on loving God. He will do anything he can to get our attention, effectively keeping us from giving our attention to God.

Spiritual warfare is essentially a battle over who gets our attention—God, or anything else. Things that we actually see, like someone being controlled by a demon, are simply effects of that person being so distracted from God that he or she actually focuses on and pays attention to Satan, giving him a place in his or her life.

For those who haven't given their lives to God, Satan fights to keep deceiving so that they never do. He wants to drag them down with him. On the other side, he has no direct control over those who have given their lives to God, because they have the Holy Spirit with them. However, he does everything he can to keep them from being effective in living their lives for God. It is how he fights those of us who have given our lives to God that I want to focus on for the rest of the chapter.

There are lies that several of us in the church have allowed ourselves to believe. These lies come from Satan, who seeks to get the church to focus on the wrong things and thus become ineffective at spreading the love of God to a world that needs to hear about it.

I am going to look at three lies that we in the church have allowed to deceive us (there are more, but to keep this chapter from becoming a book unto itself I'm just looking at these three). Please make sure that you read all the lies I address, even if you don't believe you struggle with one. You might and just not know it.

Lie 1: God Wants All Christians to Be Healthy and Wealthy

To me this is one of the weirdest of all the lies that people in the church believe. If you read the Bible at all, you'll see that there is not much in there about God wanting us to be healthy or wealthy.

1 Peter 1:15–16 says, "Therefore, prepare your minds for action; be self-controlled; set your hope fully on the grace to be given you when Jesus Christ is revealed. As obedient children, do not conform to the evil desires you had when you lived in ignorance. But just as he who called you is holy, so be holy in all you do; for it is written: 'Be holy, because I am holy'" (NIV).

God cares not that we have everything we want here on this earth, but rather that we live lives that are holy in his sight. We are to be holy just like he is holy. Ephesians 5:1 tells us that we are to be imitators of God. Since God is holy, we also are to be holy. If you want to know how to be like God, just follow the example of Jesus Christ when he was on the earth.

Jesus was not rich, never lived comfortably, and never preached that we should be comfortable. In fact, Jesus literally told us to expect suffering and hard times. In John 16:33 he warned us that in this world we would have trouble, and in Luke 21:17 he said that men would hate us because of Him. What Jesus did call us to was a life of sacrifice for God and others. In the story of the rich young ruler that I mentioned in a previous chapter, Jesus told him that he had to sell all his possessions or give them to the poor.

This lie that God wants us to be healthy and wealthy has led many astray. It has caused many to focus solely on getting financially secure, and when that is their focus, it leads to a lack of necessary faith in God. It has led to beliefs that teach if you are sick or suffering physically, it is because you have sinned. Yet when we read the book of Job, we find out that even those who are considered "blameless in the sight of God" can suffer greatly. Job's friends told him that he must have sinned, but that was not the case.

God isn't interested in just giving us money, possessions, health, or comfort. God is interested in us being willing as followers of Christ to sacrifice everything for the sake of living for and obeying him and his Word.

When we focus on this lie, we miss the truth that we are to be holy as he was holy. We forget that we are to sacrifice everything for God. We focus on ourselves and what our flesh wants, and we take our focus off God—and that is Satan's strategy.

Lie 2: Church Is All About Me and What I Want

Every church has one thing in common: there are people in it. With people come opinions, preferences, likes, and dislikes. The more people you have, the more opinions, preferences, likes, and dislikes you will have.

Now, there is nothing wrong with having personal opinions and preferences. God created each of us to like and dislike different things. That is one thing that makes each of us unique. However, when we gather together for church, we have to put those personal preferences aside in order to work together to glorify God as a church.

In Luke 11:17, Jesus says, "Any kingdom divided against itself will be ruined, and a house divided against itself will fall" (NIV). We as the church have a purpose to glorify God and do what we can to reach the world for God. But if we are spending the majority of our time dealing with everyone's personal preferences and their complaints about things that don't fit their preferences, we can't be unified and won't be able to accomplish our goal of glorifying God and reaching the world for him. We will be a divided church, and when we are divided, we will be ruined and will fall.

When a church works together as a whole toward a common goal to glorify God and reach the world, it will be a light to this dark world. But when people begin to regularly bring up what they don't like or how they'd do it differently, that light will be hidden from the world.

Church is a place where we as followers of Christ gather together and put aside our differences in order to work together to glorify God in our lives and reach the world around us for God. When church becomes anything else, we spend our time focusing on the wrong things—and that is Satan's strategy.

Lie 3: We Are the Judges of This World

Now, I bet no one would come out and say this directly, but many in the church act out this lie all the time. And often it happens under a banner of "spiritualism." For example, I've heard of Bible studies where those in attendance spend half their time talking about people who are sinners and how bad they are. They use something spiritual—a Bible study—to bash those they don't like. And what's worse is that they don't think they are doing anything wrong.

I once had someone who didn't think I dressed nice enough tell me that when we get to heaven, God will judge us based on how we dressed at church. My question for that person, as well as anyone else that believes that, is this: where do you find that in the Bible?

What would you do if I had a picture of myself right here and you saw that I had my ears pierced, a nose ring, long hair, and a tattoo on my neck? Would you begin to question whether or not you should put this book down because of how I as the author look? I don't look like that, but in all honesty it shouldn't matter.

When God told Samuel to go to Jesse's house to find the new king of Israel, this very thing came up. He got there and saw all but one of Jesse's sons. They were tall, strong, and of good stature. As far as Samuel was concerned, one of these guys was the one God wanted, because they looked so good. But God said to Samuel in 1 Samuel 16:7, "Do not consider his appearance or his height, for I have rejected him. The Lord does not look at the things man looks at. Man looks at the outward appearance, but the Lord looks at the heart" (NIV).

When we judge people, we make assumptions about them before getting to know them for who they really are. Often we will stay away from those we don't like. But that goes against the command to go into all the world and preach the good news to all creation (Mark 16:15). It says all creation, not certain creation based upon our selection criteria.

Matt 7:1–2 says, "Do not judge lest you be judged. For in the way you judge, you will be judged; and by your standard of measure, it will be measured to you" (NASB). Luke 6:36–37 tells us to "be merciful, just as your Father is merciful. And do not judge and you will not be judged; and do not condemn, and you will not be condemned; pardon, and you will be pardoned" (NASB).

When I was in high school, I went with a friend of mine to a Christian rock concert. During the show the lead singer started to pump up the crowd. He would say the name of a popular band, and we would cheer. The more popular the bands he named, the louder we cheered. Then he said Marilyn Manson, an anti-God rock band, and everyone began to boo. After a moment he quieted the crowd and said something I'll never forget: "Jesus died for Marilyn Manson too!"

We should see everyone through God's eyes, as loved and precious and created in the image of God. I could take what that band leader said and change it to anyone, and it would still be true. Jesus died for those that struggle with sexual sin, both straight and gay; Jesus died for those with tattoos and piercings as well as those who disapprove of them; Jesus died for atheists, agnostics, Mormons, etc; Jesus died for those who have spent their whole life in the church as well as those who have never set foot in one; Jesus died for those who are judgmental.

When we begin to become selective in whom we are willing to love, we begin to make God's love exclusive as well. When we begin to focus on what is outside instead of what is inside, we are withholding God's love from those who need it—and that is Satan's strategy.

So, now that we know Satan's strategy in this spiritual battle, how do we begin to fight back? How can we keep from being deceived into believing the lies?

When banks and other financial institutions want to train employees to spot a counterfeit bill, they have them study the real one. That way, when a fake one shows up, they can tell it isn't real because it doesn't look like the real thing. If they studied all the fake ones they knew of they would never be able to spot a new fake because they don't know the truth, just all the lies. To be able to spot the fake, they must first memorize the truth.

As followers of Christ, the way we fight against Satan and his lies is simple: read the Bible. That's it—no magic potion or weekend seminar or special chant. If you want to know when Satan is lying to you, you need to know the truth. To know the truth, you have to read, study, and memorize what God says in his Word, the Bible. And not just parts of the Bible—you need to become familiar with the whole thing.

When we are too busy to read our Bible, we are in that moment in the middle of spiritual warfare, because Satan is trying to distract us from focusing on God and his Word. To counter that, you have to decide that the busyness of life will not keep you from reading the Word of God and focusing on him.

Know this: Satan never rests in his attempt to distract us from God, and every area of our life is susceptible to his attacks. That is why spiritual warfare is an all-inclusive battle that involves everything in our lives. And whether we will be ready and able to fight will be determined by whether we are willing to read and know the Word of God.

Prayer

When I turned eighteen, my grandma gave me one of the greatest gifts I've ever gotten: a John Elway jersey! I am a huge fan of the Denver Broncos, and at that time John Elway was their quarterback. The week or so after my eighteenth birthday was the Super Bowl, and the Broncos were going to be playing. I loved that jersey so much that I wore it to church that Super Bowl Sunday, and I wore it all through the game, which we won!

Since then I have treated that jersey with honor. I have never washed it because I don't want to ruin it or wear it out. I only wear it on special occasions, and I always wear a shirt underneath it so that I don't get any sweat on and need to wash it. No one else is allowed to wear it, EVER! That is my jersey, and I love it and will always take care of it. It is a prized possession.

Prayer should be the same thing to us as followers of Christ. God, through the death of his son, Jesus, didn't just give us the ability to have our sins forgiven, but he also gave us the privilege of being able to communicate directly with him.

That's right. Not only did Jesus' death accomplish the cleansing of our sin if we give our lives to him, but he was also making it possible for us to come directly to God. Before that there were priests that would go before God on behalf of the people. But when Jesus died, all that changed.

Mark 15:37–38 says, "With a loud cry, Jesus breathed his last. The curtain of the temple was torn in two from top to bottom" (NIV). This curtain was what separated the rest of the temple from the Holy of Holies, the place where God dwelt and where only priests could go. At the moment of Jesus' death for our sins, this curtain was torn. It was torn from the top to the bottom, not the bottom to the top. The way it was torn was God's way of showing us that he was now allowing those who believe in what Jesus did on the cross to have direct access to God—no priests necessary.

If prayer is a privilege that was given to us by God himself, then why do we so often neglect it? Usually when someone gives us an amazing gift, we are thankful and use it often. To treat the gift of prayer with anything less than honor is like a slap in the face of God. Harsh words, but the truth is not always easy.

In 2002 and 2003, I worked full time with Youth for Christ in Omaha. I also spent a year working as the interim youth pastor at a local church in a town just south of Omaha. I lived six blocks from the church, so students could easily stop by. Often, guys would come over, and we'd play video games on my PS2. One of their favorite games to play was James Bond. In this game everyone was against everyone else, and the person who shot the other players the most would win.

Now, my favorite video game to play is Madden NFL. The object of that game and the way it is played are totally different from that of the James Bond game they would bring over. But when there were four or five people, it was easier to play the multiplayer James Bond game.

My weapon of choice in that game was the sniper rifle, mainly because it was the easiest to use. I would try to find a good hiding place and just wait for people to come into my line of sight, and then I'd pick them off. The only problem was that I was absolutely terrible at this game. It would take me a good five to ten seconds of setting my sight before I would be able to shoot, and by then they were either gone or had shot me. I never ever won a game or even came in any other place than last.

I never did well in that game because I never practiced to get better and didn't know how to properly use the weapon. That is what prayer is to most who claim to follow Christ. It is a weapon in our hands that has amazing power, but we don't really know how to use it. And too often we don't work at it so that we can use it right, so when we do use it, we continue to use it the wrong way.

Throughout the Gospels, we see that Jesus went off by himself to pray a lot. If Jesus, who was God in the flesh, needed to regularly get away and pray, then how much more do we who are not God in the flesh need to constantly pray? It is absolutely essential if we want to live a life that is pleasing to God.

Prayer is how we, as followers of Christ here on this earth, stay close to God in a world that seems to constantly be pulling us away from him. Prayer is how we keep ourselves focused when Satan is distracting us. Prayer is how we talk to our creator and savior. Prayer is the very thing we need when we don't know what to do, don't feel like going on in this struggle, get confused, or need a break and reminder of how good and amazing God is. Prayer is a privilege and an opportunity given to us through the death of Jesus.

I believe that the biggest reason many of us neglect prayer is not because we want to, but because we are ignorant when it comes to prayer. We don't fully understand the when, where, why, and how of prayer, and therefore we don't give it the priority and attention that we should.

In the rest of the chapter I want to look at the when, where, why, and how of prayer. And hopefully it will clear up some confusion and ignorance so that we, as followers of Christ, can begin to use it properly and make it a top priority in our lives.

When

1 Thessalonians 5:16–18 says, "Be joyful always; pray continually; give thanks in all circumstances, for this is God's will for you in

Christ Jesus" (NIV). You can pray whenever you want, always. There is no wrong time to pray; it is always the right time.

Often, God will place a person on my mind. When that happens, I will at that very moment say a prayer for that person, even if I don't know what he or she needs prayer for. I know that God does, so I pray that God be with that person in whatever he or she is going through at this moment and that he or she grows closer to God.

Recently I was running an errand, and an old friend of mine whom I hadn't seen or talked to in a long time popped into my head. I thought it was kind of random for him to be in my thoughts because of how long it had been since we had last talked, but I thought maybe there is a reason for that.

So I pulled out my phone and called him. I got his voicemail, so I left a quick message telling him that God had placed him on my mind and I was curious if there was anything I could pray for him about. When I hung up I quickly said a short general prayer for him, like the one mentioned above.

A minute later he called me back and proceeded to tell me that he was going through some hard things at that moment. In fact, he had just received some very serious and sad news involving a family member, and he was really struggling with it.

The day God placed him on my mind was the same day he was hit with some hard news. Coincidence? No. And if I hadn't prayed for him right when I thought about it, I very likely would have forgotten because of the busyness of the day.

Our time is already limited and often busy. Use your time wisely, and always be ready to pray.

Where

I spent a month in the summer of 1998 on a mission trip to Romania. I went with a group my mom and dad led that consisted of several high school and college-aged students. We spent a week at a camp where we, along with students from different towns and villages around Romania, were trained to do backyard Bible clubs for kids. Then those of us from America were split into different teams and sent to different towns and villages in order to work with churches there. I was in a town called Gerla with three other students and my youth pastor.

One evening after we'd finished our clubs, we decided to take a walk to the center of town so we could hang out in the park there. As we were walking, a conversation about something serious began. I don't remember what the conversation was about, but I do remember a response that one of the guys said. My youth pastor said, "Where do you stand on that?", asking what my friend thought. He immediately stopped and said, "Wherever I stop walking." We all just busted out laughing at that moment.

You don't have to be in a church building during a prayer service to pray. You don't have to be sitting down to eat a meal in order to pray. You can pray wherever you are at that moment—wherever you are standing or sitting at this exact moment.

Since whenever is a good time to pray, that implies that wherever is also a good place to pray. You can pray while sitting at your desk at work, while you are watching your kids play, and even while you are driving. You shouldn't always close your eyes, especially when doing things like driving or watching your kids, but you don't have to close your eyes to pray. Simply say a prayer in your head while you drive while keeping your focus on the road.

If we are to "pray continually," then we are going to have to always be in a mind-set that is ready to say a prayer for whatever or whomever God lays on our heart, no matter what we are doing at the time.

Why

James 5:16 tells us to "pray for one another, so that you may be healed. The effective prayer of a righteous man can accomplish much" (NASB).

Ephesians 6:18 says, "And pray in the Spirit on all occasions with all kinds of prayers and requests. With this in mind, be alert and always keep on praying for all the saints" (NIV).

Philippians 4:6 says, "Be anxious for nothing, but in everything by prayer and supplication with thanksgiving let your requests be made known to God" (NASB).

Psalms 55:22 says, "Cast your cares on the Lord and he will sustain you; he will never let the righteous fall" (NIV).

Hebrews 4:16 says, "Let us then approach the throne of grace with confidence, so that we may receive mercy and find grace to help us in our time of need" (NIV).

Matthew 9:37–38 says, "Then he said to his disciples, 'The harvest is plentiful but the workers are few. Ask the Lord of the harvest, therefore, to send out workers into his harvest field'" (NIV).

Need I say anything more?

How

In Matthew 6:9–13, Jesus gave his disciples a sample prayer. It says, "This, then, is how you should pray: 'Our Father in heaven, hallowed be your name, your kingdom come, your will be done on earth as it is in heaven. Give us today our daily bread. Forgive us our debts, as we also have forgiven our debtors. And lead us not into temptation, but deliver us from the evil one'" (NIV).

This prayer begins by praising God ("Our Father in heaven, hallowed be your name") and then goes straight into seeking God's will ("your kingdom come, your will be done on earth as it is in heaven"). After that the attention turns to the person doing the prayer, but not in the way we often do. The attention is given to the basic survival needs of the person ("give us today our daily bread") and then to our sinful state and the need for forgiveness ("forgive us our debts as we also have forgiven our debtors"). And then finally there is a plea from the person to God for strength to stay away from temptation so that we won't fall into sin ("And lead us not into temptation, but deliver us from the evil one").

Look back at Jesus' example prayer. Then think about how you pray. Do you start off by praising God? Do you focus on how amazing God is and pray that his will would be done instead of yours? Do you pray for your basic survival needs, or do you pray more for your wish list? Do you pray that God would forgive you as you forgive others, or do you ask God to forgive you even though you refuse to forgive others, making forgiveness all about you? Do you pray for strength to stay away from evil, or do you rely on yourself for that and only remember to pray after you've failed?

In Jesus' prayer there is little focus on what we want and much focus on what God wants. But in most of our prayers there is little focus on God's will and much focus on what we want. That is using prayer the wrong way.

We need to pray for God's will to be done when it comes to everything. And when we do, we need to be willing to accept the fact that God's will might not fit what we want but that his will is better than ours.

1 John 5:14–16 says, "And this is the confidence which we have before him, that, if we ask anything according to his will, he hears us. And if we know that he hears us in whatever we ask, we know that we have the requests which we have asked from him" (NASB).

Many see that last phrase "we have the requests which we have asked from him" and take it to mean that God will give us anything we ask for that we want. But earlier in those verses it says "if we ask anything according to His will, He hears us." His will, not ours.

One of the phrases that I hear most often from people when they pray is this: "Help us to have a good day today." That phrase has always bothered me, because it is not praying for God's will at all. Like I mentioned in the last chapter, God is not just out to make us comfortable. He is interested in making us holy just like he is. Instead of praying for a good day, we should be praying that God would use us to accomplish his will, even if that means we have to go through something hard.

He wants us to pray for his will for this world. He wants us to pray for our family and friends who aren't followers of Christ to come to him. He wants us to pray for the gospel to make it to every tribe, tongue, and nation—and just remember that you might be the answer to that prayer. He wants us to pray that followers of Christ would continue to follow him, no matter what. He wants us to put others needs before our own in our prayers. He wants us to seek him and his will, not our will.

At the beginning of the chapter I mentioned my grandma. For several years my grandma had been very sick, and we had been praying for healing as well as that God would take care of her during that time. After a long time of being sick, she passed away.

Many would take that as God not answering our prayer, but that is how we see the situation if what we are praying for is our will. To us on earth, healing means that she is healed here on this earth. Yet if we look at it from God's point of view, he totally answered our prayer. Grandma had been sick for a long time. God did heal her, just not in the way we would have thought.

My grandma is now in a place described in Revelation 21:4 as a place where "He will wipe every tear from their eyes. There will be no more death or mourning or crying or pain, for the old order of things has passed away" (NIV). She is in heaven now, in the presence of God himself, and she will never feel pain or suffering again. God totally healed her; he just healed her differently than we often think.

When we care more about God's will than our own, what we pray for is going to be for God's will to happen. Putting God and his will first in our lives leads us to grow in righteous. And when a righteous man prays, it is for the will of God to be accomplished.

Forgiveness

There is a scene in *Spiderman 3* when Peter Parker is under the control of black Spiderman (you'd understand if you saw the movie) and confronts Eddie Brock, another photojournalist at the newspaper where he works. The confrontation is about a photo turned in that is a fake. Eddie Brock says to Peter, "When are you gonna give a guy a break?" Peter responds, "You want forgiveness? Get religion!"

Man, don't I wish that statement were true! I wish that people looking for forgiveness for a mistake they've made could come to a church and that church would show them God's love and forgiveness. I wish that people would feel so loved by the church that it would become where they turn in times of trouble, and through the church they would find God. I wish, I wish, I wish.

What's sad is that far too often that wish does not come true. Way too often those who are in the church decide to condemn and shun those who've sinned and are in need of forgiveness. When that happens, we often end up chasing people away from God instead of moving them toward God.

It has always amazed and disgusted me when those in the church, who've accepted the forgiveness of God in their own lives, are not willing to give that same forgiveness to others. They are so willing to accept forgiveness for themselves, but then they decide to keep it to themselves and not share it with others who need it too. It's pathetic!

The hardest thing about this is that there are times that I'm no different because I can struggle with this as well, and the place I'm reminded of this struggle the most is in my marriage. My wife might say something to me that I don't like or treat me in a way that makes me feel bad. I'll get upset, we'll eventually talk about, and she'll ask for forgiveness. I'll say that I forgive her, but if I'm completely honest, I don't always really forgive her.

I don't really forgive her because I don't forget what she did or how she made me feel. I might let it go for that time, but I will file that feeling away in my mind. And when she does something else I will pull out that other thing and remind myself—and sometimes even remind her—of that past offense as well as the present one. If I remember what she did to me in the past and use it against her ever again, either by telling her or by letting it affect how I treat her, then I haven't truly forgiven her of that offense.

Forgiveness, true complete forgiveness, cannot happen without forgetting the offense. Forgiveness and forgetfulness go hand in hand. You can't have the first without the second.

Psalm 103:8–12 says, "The Lord is compassionate and gracious, slow to anger, abounding in love. He will not always accuse, nor will he harbor his anger forever; he does not treat us as our sins deserve or repay us according to our iniquities. For as high as the heavens are above the earth, so great is his love for those who fear him; as far as the east is from the west, so far has he removed our transgressions from us" (NIV).

What a beautiful passage that describes the love and forgiveness of God. My favorite part of that passage is the last phrase, where it says "as far as the east is from the west, so far has he removed our transgressions from us." How far is the east from the west? At what point do you stop traveling east and start traveling west? You don't. As long as you travel east you will continue to travel east. And as long as you travel west you will continue to do so. There is no east or west pole like there is a north and south pole.

What that phrase means is that God gets rid of our sin. He literally puts it in a place that you can't get to. He, in effect, forgets about it. The sin is gone, forever. He will never accuse you of that sin or make you feel guilty about it again. It is gone. If you ever feel guilty about a past sin that you've confessed, it is not God who is doing that. It is either Satan trying to lie to you or it is you not forgiving yourself.

If it is Satan, then you know how to fight back: hold onto the truth found in Scripture that says God puts your sin as far as the east is from the west. Remind yourself of that verse and that truth, and you will be able to fight against Satan's lie.

If it is you not forgiving yourself, then my question is this: why won't you? Do you believe that God would lie to you in his word when he says he forgives you and gets rid of it? If God is willing to forgive you for that sin, then accept it with gladness and forgive yourself as well. After all, who are we to argue with God?

1 Peter 3:18 tells us, "For Christ also died for sins once for all, the just for the unjust, so that He might bring us to God" (NASU). When Christ died for our sins, God was giving us a way to have our sins forgiven once and for all. Before Christ's sacrifice, in order to be forgiven for your sin, you had to make continual animal sacrifices on the altar. When Christ died, he put the need for continual sacrifices aside and made it possible for us to have our sins forgiven with one sacrifice.

I think that often we as followers of Christ don't fully realize what that verse is telling us. I know that I only recently began to understand it fully. It says that "Christ died for sins once for all." And if you look back in Psalm 103, you'll see that is says that God removes our sin "as far as the east is from the west." If we are to take those verses for what they say, then once we've given our lives to Christ and asked him to forgive our sins, that is it. He has "once for all" forgiven all of our sin, not just the sin leading up to when we asked for forgiveness and began to follow him.

But that is often how we see it. We think that when we give our lives to Christ and ask for his forgiveness for our sins, he forgives what we've done so far. But then after that we have to confess each sin to him so that he will again forgive us. Yet if I look at the two verses mentioned above, I don't see that at all. What I see is complete and total forgiveness for every sin I have ever committed or ever will commit. What an awesome truth!

1 John 1:9–2:2 says, "If we confess our sins, he is faithful and just and will forgive us our sins and purify us from all unrighteousness. If we claim we have not sinned, we make him out to be a liar and his word has no place in our lives. My dear children, I write this to you so that you will not sin. But if anybody does sin, we have one who speaks to the Father in our defense—Jesus Christ, the Righteous One. He is the atoning sacrifice for our sins, and not only for ours but also for the sins of the whole world" (NIV).

When we are willing to recognize that we are sinners and confess our sins to God, he will forgive us. And when we do sin after that, "we have one who speaks to the Father in our defense—Jesus." What does he say? Jesus defends us to God, letting him know that our sins have already been forgiven; we are clean because of Jesus' sacrifice on the cross.

So does that mean we should never ask God to forgive us when we do sin? No, we definitely should. But not in the same way we did when we first confessed our sins to him and chose to follow him. Instead we should look at it more like when we have to apologize to a person we are in relationship with. When we wrong someone that we have a relationship with, that relationship becomes strained, hurt, and even divided. To fix it we have to apologize for what we did and mend those strains, hurts, and divisions.

When I wrong my wife, our relationship shows it. So it is up to me, the person who did the wronging, to go and fix my mistake. When I do, we can put it behind us and move forward in a good relationship instead of struggling forward in a bad one.

When we give our lives to God and ask for forgiveness of our sins, we begin a relationship with God. That relationship, if it is true and sincere, will never break apart, because we are told in Hebrews 13:5 that God will never leave us. There is no divorce in this relationship; it is forever. So we as followers of Christ must then work at keeping that relationship strong. Since God is perfect we will always be the ones in the wrong, which means we have to be the ones that work to fix it and keep it repaired.

Now that we understand the degree and depth to which we have been forgiven, we need to begin to show that same forgiveness to others around us because they need it too. Ephesians 4:32 says, "Be kind and compassionate to one another, forgiving each other, just as in Christ God forgave you" (NIV).

According to that verse, we are to forgive other people the same way that God forgives us. That means when we forgive other people for what they've done, we remove it as far as the east is from the west. We are to forget about it, let it go, and never bring it up again or let it affect how we treat that person.

This does not mean that when certain sins are committed, a relationship won't change. In fact, there are times when a relationship should change because of a wrong that is committed. Yet even when things go wrong and the dynamics of a relationship change, true forgiveness is still possible. We are to still forgive just as God forgives us.

Because we as humans are diverse, have different perspectives, and are imperfect, we will all at some point do something to someone else that hurts him or her or causes a rift in our relationship. That is just the fact of being imperfect and different from each other. However, just because that is the case that does not let us off the hook of making sure we make right our wrongs.

Romans 12:18 says, "If it is possible, as far as it depends on you, live at peace with everyone" (NIV). To live at peace with all, we have to be willing to forgive and forget. When we hold a grudge, we don't live at peace. When our lack of forgiveness keeps us from loving someone like we should, the relationship is hurt, and we disobey God's commands.

In all honesty, true forgiveness is one of the hardest things to do. It is very difficult for us as humans to actually forget what someone else has done to us. We are people who remember things so that we won't be hurt again. It is a part of self-preservation, and we all do it. Yet to truly forgive like God says we should, it requires us to put aside our nature as humans and live in God's strength.

Remember this: Galatians 5:1 says, "It is for freedom that Christ has set us free. Stand firm, then, and do not let yourselves be burdened again by a yoke of slavery" (NIV). Jesus didn't die for us so that we could continue to hold sins against ourselves and others. We are no longer slaves to sin, so do not act like it anymore. Jesus died so that we would truly be free in the way we live.

Allow yourself to be free from sin, because God has forgiven you. Free yourself from creating divisions in your relationship with other people—and pass that freedom along to the rest of the world as well. After all, Jesus died to set everyone free.

Relationships

When I was working in Omaha, I would go every summer to our district high school camp. Since I was a youth pastor in the district, I had several responsibilities and duties during that week. I loved going to camp! It is so much fun to spend a week every year with a ton of high school students, playing games, hearing great speakers, and building relationships on all different levels.

In the summer of 2007, our camp director decided that we would do something a little different at camp. One evening, toward the end of the week, we were going to have what he called a "blessing service." He went on to explain that a blessing service is a time set aside when we as leaders would have the opportunity to speak encouragement and/or prayer into a student's life; we would bless him or her with our words.

I was very intrigued by this idea, because I had never been a part of anything like it. I was also a little nervous thinking about speaking blessings into these students' lives, some of whom I didn't even know. But I liked the idea, so I was willing to give it a shot and see how it turned out. As that evening approached, I got more anxious and excited about it.

After the evening chapel, the camp director dismissed the students to go to their cabins to put their stuff away, go the bathroom, etc. They were then to head down to the cafeteria for this blessing service. As they went back to their cabins, we as leaders went to the cafeteria and got ready. We moved all the chairs and tables to the side, and then we spread out around the outside walls of the room. A few minutes later all the students came in, not really sure of what was about to happen (just like us leaders). They sat down on the floor in the middle of the room and looked around the room, trying to figure out what was going on.

Once all the students had been seated, the camp director explained how this would work. Students, whenever they wanted to, could get up and go to the leader of their choosing to receive a word of blessing from that leader. If another student was with that leader, they would form a line and wait their turn. Students sitting and not going to leaders were asked to be respectful and stay quiet. This service would last as long as students were going up to leaders, so there was no time limit or rush. After all the explanations were done, it was time to begin.

No one moved. We as leaders stood there looking at the students, and the students sat on the floor looking at each other. No one was really sure what to do for a moment because this was such a new concept for so many.

Then it happened. Slowly, one of the students stood up and walked over to a leader. And as soon as that student led off, it was as if we had released cattle from their pen. Students all over the room stood up and started walking to different leaders.

As the first student walked toward me, the nerves really hit. What do I say? How do I stand? I suddenly became very aware of my hands, which is something that happens when I'm nervous. Do I cross my arms? No, that would make me look mad. Do I fold my hands in front of me? Do I put them in my pockets? AHHH!

The first student that walked up to me was one of the students from my church, so that made me a little more comfortable. I don't really remember what I said or how I said it; I just remember praying for that student, who then walked off to another leader. After that, another student came up to me. I spoke with that student and then prayed for her. And then another student came, and then another and another.

When I had a moment for a quick break, I took a look around the room and saw that students were all over the place talking with the different leaders. At that moment I became very overwhelmed with what was happening in that room. These students, many of them now in tears, were not used to being blessed. It was not a regular occurrence for them to have someone say something encouraging to them and then pray for them.

We as humans are very harsh with our words. The phrase "sticks and stones may break my bones, but words will never hurt me" is such a huge lie. Words can hurt very much, sometimes even more than sticks and stones. We even joke in mean ways with our friends. Encouraging people has become so abnormal that when we encounter it, we don't really know how to act. I even have to tell my wife at times to just say thank you when I give her a compliment.

This blessing service continued on like this for three hours! Three hours of students receiving words of encouragement and prayer. As it was finally winding down, my emotions were shot from all that had happened in there. I had experienced what Hebrews 3:13 tells us in a very real way, and my emotions couldn't take much more. The Holy Spirit was truly working in that place! Then, as if what I had experienced wasn't enough, one of my students walked up to me and proceeded to bless me and pray for me.

That put it over the top. I was so overwhelmed with everything that I literally couldn't stand anymore. I sat down on the floor with tears streaming down my face as I watched students and leaders begin to head back to their cabins. Few things have ever touched me the way that night did, and it became my favorite part of camp the following years. It also became a favorite among the students, who would request every year that we have it again.

Hebrews 3:13 says, "But encourage one another day after day, as long as it is still called 'Today,' lest any one of you be hardened by the deceitfulness of sin" (NASB). So many people have hard hearts because of hurtful words spoken to them, and when our hearts are hardened, we become more susceptible to falling into sin. To keep that from happening, we need to speak words of encouragement on a daily basis. If we obey what the Bible says, then what took place in that blessing service should be a normal thing in our churches and homes. But it isn't, and that is what makes an experience like that so overwhelming. Deep down, we know that this is how it is supposed to be, and our hearts begin to soften again because we know it is right.

I can say with complete confidence that if you are reading this book, you are in a relationship, and probably many different relationships of varying degrees. We are all different in many ways, but one thing we all in common is that we know what a relationship is and that we are currently in one.

When I say in a relationship, I don't just mean a boyfriend-girlfriend or marriage relationship; I mean any relationship. If you have friends, then you are in a friendship relationship. If you have family, then you are part of a family relationship. If you ever go outside your own home, then you have some acquaintance relationships. Work, school, church, social club, etc—relationships are everywhere, and we are a part of them.

The problem with relationships is that they are not easy. In the last chapter I talked about how we are always the one at fault in our relationship with God because he is perfect. But here on this earth, our relationships are between two or more people who are all imperfect, which means more issues to deal with and a need for forgiveness on everyone's part.

Many, if not all, of us have been in a relationship where we are doing everything we know to keep the peace and treat the other person well, but the other person does not treat us that way in return. When that happens, our tendency is to start treating that person the way he or she is treating us. After all, the other person deserves it, since he or she is treating us wrong.

Matthew 7:12 says, "So in everything, do to others what you would have them do to you, for this sums up the Law and the Prophets" (NIV). Ever hear of the Golden Rule? This is where it comes from. We are to treat others the way we want them to treat us. There is no stipulation in that verse that says if they don't treat you right, then you can treat them wrong too. The command is clear: you do what is right even if the other person doesn't.

Matthew 22:37–40 says, "Love the Lord your God with all your heart and with all your soul and with all your mind. This is the first and greatest commandment. And the second is like it: Love your neighbor as yourself. All the Law and the Prophets hang on these two commandments" (NIV).

The common denominator in the two greatest commandments is love. We are to love God and love others. 1 John 4:21 tells us the same thing: "And he has given us this command: Whoever loves God must also love his brother" (NIV). Our love for other people is connected to our love for God.

I think it's safe to say that loving other people is very important to God. When we treat others the way we'd like them to treat us, even if they don't, that showing them love. And when we love them, we love God because we are obeying him.

Earlier I mentioned that there are varying degrees of relationships: friends, coworkers, family, acquaintances, etc. But the ultimate relationship on this earth is marriage. In a marriage you live together, buy things together, plan your future together, make decisions together, have a family together, budget together, etc. Marriage is the relationship that is 24/7/365—even when you are asleep, you are still together in the same bed.

The thing we need to realize about marriage is that God uses marriage to give us a living example of our relationship with him. Remember that loving God and loving others are connected to each other, and marriage is that ultimate relationship that tests our love and allows us to express our love in ways we shouldn't in any of our other relationships.

Ephesians 5:31–33 says, "'For this reason a man will leave his father and mother and be united to his wife, and the two will become one flesh.' This is a profound mystery—but I am talking about Christ and the church. However, each one of you also must love his wife as he loves himself, and the wife must respect her husband" (NIV).

I want to look at three different things in these verses because they are so key to understanding the relationship of marriage that God has given us.

First of all, Paul, the author of these verses, intertwines God and marriage. He says that he is talking about Christ and the church in the midst of talking about the marriage relationship. To really see this, read verses 21–33 and notice how many times Paul jumps from the marriage relationship to God and back again. It is as if Paul can't mention marriage without referring to God. Just like in 1 John 4:21 when we saw that loving God means we must love others; this is another example of how our relationships here on earth are connected to our relationship with God.

Marriage is supposed to be an example of what our relationship with God should be like. A marriage relationship is God's way of showing us how to be in a close intimate relationship with him. It is also his way of giving us a barometer of our relationship with him. If we are neglecting our spouse, not loving him or her well or striving to continue to grow in that relationship, then that shows us where we are spiritually as well. As it says in 1 John 4:20, if we can't love those around us, whom we can see, then we can't love God, whom we can't see.

Secondly, we are shown how men are to treat their wives and how wives are to treat their husbands. Men are to love their wives, and wives are to respect their husbands. That's interesting to me, because my human mind would say that we are to love each other. But God knows us so well that he knows how we truly feel loved.

Women want to feel loved, adored, honored, and cherished. That is how God created women, and that is what they care about most. Men, on the other hand, care more about feeling respected than loved. I know this because I am a man and would say that I want to know that my wife respects me much more than I want to know that she loves me. When she shows me respect, then I feel loved. But when I don't feel respected, I don't feel loved, no matter how much she says she loves me.

In that verse, we are commanded to love our spouses the way they want to be loved. We are to make their needs our top priority; we are to put them first.

Thirdly, it says that "a man will leave his father and mother and be united to his wife, and the two will become one flesh." There is a progression in that verse that unfortunately is often ignored. A man goes on his own, becoming a man. Then when he's a man, which implies maturity, he gets married. *Wife* is a legal term that comes out of a marriage ceremony. And once that marriage ceremony has taken place and the woman is that man's wife, then the two will become one flesh (that's talking about sex). It goes maturity, marriage, and then sex. That is the way God intended it.

God is so serious about it being in that order, with sex coming into the equation after marriage, that in Exodus 22:16 it says: "If a man seduces a virgin who is not pledged to be married and sleeps with her, he must pay the bride-price, and she shall be his wife" (NIV). This command was given to Israel long ago. God gave the Israelites these kinds of commands so they would know how to live for him, as well as to ensure they looked and acted different from the world around them.

We are to look and act different from the world around us as well, so that means we also must see sex the way God does. Sex and marriage go together; the two are not to be separated. Sex is only to take place in marriage because marriage is the only relationship sex is intended for. And since God is the one that gave us sex, we should look at it from his point of view. Sex is the ultimate expression of love and respect and honor in the ultimate relationship, marriage.

Like I said before, relationships are not always easy—but they are very important. If we claim to love God, then we have to love others; that is just the way it is. If you don't like it, talk to God, because he is the one that made it that way.

Philippians 2:3 says, "Do nothing from selfishness or empty conceit, but with humility of mind let each of you regard one another as more important than himself" (NASB). The best relationships are the ones where each person is putting the other before him- or herself. If you want others to do that for you, then according to Matthew 7:12, you have to do it first.

It is this very truth that God has been working on in me for a while now, both in my marriage relationship as well as in all my other relationships. I have been learning—sometimes way too slowly, unfortunately—to be encouraging to others and to put others first.

As I've been learning these lessons, I decided to institute two "days" in my life to ensure that I am applying this in my life regularly.

The first is what I call "Charissa Day." This is a day set aside each week that I try to make sure to do something special for my wife as a way to show her that I love her. It's usually not anything major; many times it's something like writing her a special note, getting her one of those fancy drinks at Starbucks, allowing her to get away for a while to be by herself without the kids (she's a stay-at-home mother who homeschools our four children), or something like that. There are times that we will go out on a date, but since I'm in ministry and she stays home, money is tight, and thus I have to be more creative most of the time. This is just a simple way to remind me to put her first and to regularly show her that I love her.

The second is what I call "Encouragement Day." I have a day and time set on my phone's calendar, and each week on that day at that time my alarm goes off to notify me that it's Encouragement Day. This is a day when I intentionally say something encouraging and uplifting to several different people. It usually takes me around fifteen to twenty minutes to write and send several encouraging notes that day, but the effect lasts all week. Those I encourage are grateful and often say something encouraging to me in return, and it helps me remember to put others before myself.

Those are just two simple ways in which I try to make sure to apply what God tells me in Scripture concerning how I am to treat others. I share those with you as a way to both encourage and challenge you to do something similar to ensure that you treat others the way God says to as well.

Love others the way you would love yourself if you were them. Look for the good in others, not the bad. Find the positive in them, not the negative. Build them up; don't tear them down. Treat them the way you would want to be treated. Love them the way God has commanded us to.

Truth

Wwe live in an age that says what you believe may be good for you, but it doesn't have to be the same for me. I can believe what I want, you can believe what you want, and we are both right because it is what works for each of us. This type of thinking is called relativism, and is a nothing more than a lie from Satan. He doesn't want anyone to know the truth that is found in the Bible, so he deceives us to see truth as relative.

The definition of *truth* is "conformity with fact or reality; a verified or indisputable fact, proposition, principle, or the like; actuality or actual existence" (dictionary.com). Truth is truth. Whether or not we choose to believe it doesn't change the fact that truth is truth. Our ideas and beliefs do not change truth. Truth has always been and will always be the same.

A simple yet effective example of this is the truth that two of anything plus two more of anything has always equaled four of that thing. No matter how much I would want to believe or try to convince others that two plus two equals seven, it wouldn't be true. Two plus two will always equal four. That's just the way it is, because that is the truth, period.

This very same idea can be applied to God and the truth of his Word as well. Hebrews 13:8 says, "Jesus Christ is the same yesterday and today and forever" (NIV). If Jesus, who is God, is the same yesterday and today and forever, then it stands to reason that the truth he created when he created the world is also the same yesterday and today and forever.

Instead of trying to make the truth fit with my life and way of thinking, I need to make my life and way of thinking fit with the truth. I can't change the facts or reality of what is the truth; I can only decide whether or not I will align my life with the truth.

The church needs to do the same thing: align itself with the truth found in Scripture. It only makes sense, since those in the church claim to be following Christ. But unfortunately, there are a lot of instances when the church has traded the truth of Scripture for the convenience of personal preference and thought.

Examples of this can be seen when the people of a church are afraid to step out in faith and do something God is leading them to do because of a handful of people who don't like the idea, when a church only focuses on God blessing them and fails to challenge the people to be holy as God is holy, when a church stops having prayer meetings because people are busy with other things, or when a church wants to hide and ignore the sin and struggle of its people rather than properly addressing it while loving those who are struggling, because ignoring and hiding it is easier.

There are many more examples of this happening in the church (too many to list), both in major and minor ways. But anytime the church trades the truth of Scripture for the convenience of personal preference and thought, it goes against the will of God and hinders its ability to minister, both inside and outside the church. When the church separates itself from the truth of Scripture, it begins to separate itself from Jesus, who referred to himself as 'the way, the TRUTH, and the life' (John 14:6). And once that happens, can we even call it a church anymore? Is it really anything more than just a social club at that point?

When I was twelve years old, God placed on my life the calling to be a youth pastor, and that has been my dream ever since. In fact, I've never wanted to do anything else in the church except work with junior high and high school students and their parents (family should be a big part of youth ministry).

So as I grew up, I began to follow my youth pastors around in order to learn from them. When I was in high school, my youth pastor, Paul Miceli, allowed me to be a part of leading youth group at times. He even let me teach a few lessons so that I could get experience. I would often spend time with him just watching how he did things and learning from his actions. He was a big mentor to me as I worked toward accomplishing this dream that God had given me.

Then I went to college to study to become a youth pastor. After about two years of college, I came to the point where I was ready to quit school, leave the church, and never become a youth pastor at all. I had found out, as I grew up and became more involved in the politics of the church, that I didn't like how a lot of people who claimed to follow Christ acted. One of my professors actually had to force me to step back from the church I was currently working in as the youth pastor on a volunteer basis. That was not an easy time for me, but if my professor had not forced me to step back, I very possibly might not be a youth pastor today. I needed to recharge and refocus myself before everything was destroyed.

During the summer between my sophomore and junior years, I decided to stay at school instead of going home. And it was through two experiences that God both renewed and rejuvenated me to continue following his will for my life to become a youth pastor.

It all started when I decided to get my tongue pierced. I knew that once school started, I would have to take it out, because the school I attended didn't allow piercings at that time, but I had always wanted to have a piercing. My current job didn't allow guys to have piercings that could be seen, so I figured that as long as I didn't talk with my mouth wide open I could hide it.

The first thing that happened involved people in the church. I knew that some wouldn't be fans of what I had done, but I never expected the reactions I got. Some people wouldn't talk to me anymore; others just looked at me with disappointed and disapproving looks. I even received a letter from someone I'd known for a long time. In this letter, I was blasted as rebelling against God, shaming my parents, and living in sin. It was a very harsh letter with a tone of almost hatred in it. I was so shocked at how I was treated because of a metal thing in my mouth.

The second thing that happened involved my boss. I was working at Embassy Suites as a valet driver—a sweet job because of all the awesome cars I got to drive. One day that summer, my boss came up to me and asked if I'd like to join him on a private valet job. Someone who worked at the hotel was getting married and wanted to pay a couple of us to do valet at the wedding. I had nothing better to do and could use the money, so I said I would help.

Now, before I continue, let me briefly tell you about my boss. He used to ride dirt bikes professionally until he blew out his knee, he liked death metal music, and he was completely against religion. Not only was he against it, he was very vocal about it. All of us who worked with him knew how much he wanted nothing to do with God because of how much he hated religion.

So the day came around when we were doing this wedding. I met him at work and rode with him to the wedding. As we were driving, we began to talk. I don't remember how it started, but we got to the topic of religion. He knew that I was going to a Christian college and studying to be a youth pastor, and obviously I knew how he felt about religion.

At one point in the conversation, he looked at me and said in a very stern and loud voice, "I can't stand religion!" Without missing a beat, I looked at him and said, "Me too!" My response really caught him off-guard because he thought that I was all about religion since I was going to a Christian college. So he gave me the chance to explain my answer.

I told him that Christianity, true Christianity, is not a religion; it's a relationship with God and a lifestyle that we live. I told him that God can't stand religion, either, because the rules and regulations associated with religion get in the way of a genuine relationship with him. I was able to share with my boss about how Jesus had died for our sins and three days later had risen again, defeating sin and death for us. I was able to share the gospel with my boss, the man who hated religion and wanted nothing to do with God, and he was actually listening. I wish I could say that my boss accepted

Christ that day, but he didn't. But I can say that he heard the truth, perhaps for the first time.

Those two experiences that summer stuck with me and really made me think. When I had my tongue pierced, those in the church shunned me. In complete contrast, someone who was completely against religion and wanted nothing to do with God was willing to listen to me, tongue ring and all. Through those two experiences, I came to realize that this world needs to be shown the truth, and the church needs to be reminded of it. So that summer I rededicated myself to seeking the truth and then sharing it, both inside and outside the church.

For far too long now we have allowed our vision to be blurred by our preferences, human eyes, and Satan's lies. It is time that we as followers of Christ hit the defrost button so that we can see out the windshield properly. We need to clear up our vision so that we can correctly proclaim God to a world of people looking for something more than what they see in front of them.

People in the world are looking for answers to their questions, and we have them in the Bible. But we can't tell them the answers until we know what the Bible says and actually live it out in our own lives.

No matter what culture you live in, no matter what denomination of church you belong to, no matter how old or young you are, if you claim to be a follower of Christ, you have the same mission that everyone else has: "Therefore go and make disciples of all nations, baptizing them in the name of the Father and of the Son and of the Holy Spirit, and teaching them to obey everything I have commanded you. And surely I am with you always, to the very end of the age" (Matthew 28:19–20, NIV).

As my youth pastor used to say, "You may be the only Jesus some people ever see. What kind of Jesus are you showing them?"

The truth is that there is a lost and dying world right outside your door, and God's plan is to have his church show them his love through both words and actions. The world needs to know that Jesus died for them so that they can have their sins forgiven. We know that those who don't have their sins forgiven will spend eternity in hell, completely separated from God.

It's time for the followers of Christ to begin living for God the way we are supposed to. It is time for the church to make the truth found in Scripture more important than the convenience of our personal preference and thought. It won't always be easy, but remember that the last thing Jesus said before returning to heaven is that he will be with us.

May we know the truth, believe the truth, proclaim the truth, and live the truth. May our vision be clear so that we may be followers of Christ who look and act just like Jesus; who are the imitation of Christ in this world, sharing God's love, forgiveness, and salvation; who are free from the bondage of sin, living a life of freedom as Christ intended; and who show everyone what it looks like to be a new creation in Christ (2 Corinthians 5:17).

The challenge is that we as followers of Christ would seek the truth of scripture so that we can live accordingly. Knowing the truth isn't enough; we have to live it out. Knowledge is useless without proper application.

So what will you do? How will you apply the truth of Scripture to your life? What will you have to change in your thinking and living so that you can align your life with the truth? Where is your vision blurred, and what will you do to clear it up?

In College, Aaron "Woogy" Wolgamott majored in both *Christian Education of Youth* and *Biblical Studies*. He has been in full-time ministry for ten years, currently serving as the Associate Pastor of Youth Ministries at Calvary Bible Church in Derry, New Hampshire. He and his wife, Charissa, have been married for eight years, and they have four children, Noah, Ali, Hope, and Kate. He loves spending time with his students, going on dates with his wife, playing with his kids, and anything to do with football. A quote by Ron Brown really describes his focus and passion in life: "I'm not afraid of failure, I'm afraid of being successful at things that don't matter."